The Brat Stops Here!

DATE DUE	

ALSO BY MARY-ELAINE JACOBSEN, Psy.D.

The Gifted Adult

MARY-ELAINE JACOBSEN, Psy.D.

The Brat
Stops Here!

5 Weeks (or Less) to

No More Tantrums, Arguing,

or Bad Behavior

St. Martin's Griffin ⚏ New York

www.stmartins.com

Library of Congress Cataloging-in-Publication Data

Jacobsen, Mary-Elaine.
    The brat stops here! : 5 weeks (or less) to no more tantrums, arguing, or
bad behavior / Mary-Elaine Jacobsen—1st ed.
        p. cm.
    Includes bibliographical references and index.
    ISBN 0-312-34279-9
    EAN 978-0-312-34279-1
    1. Problem children—Behavior modification. 2. Discipline of children. 3.
Parent and child. I. Title.

HQ773.J33 2006
649'.64—dc22   2005054366

First Edition: February 2006

10   9   8   7   6   5   4   3   2   1

To Ross, Chrissie, and Todd—

their mother's dream-come-true;

and

to loving parents everywhere

dedicated to raising their children well

[Contents]

PART I

Week 1: Understanding Temperament and Bad Behavior

PART II

Week 2: How Children Manipulate Situations and Dodge Responsibility

PART III

Week 3: Good Behavior Required Here

PART IV

Week 4: The *Dr. J Way*:
Privileges "On"/Privileges "Off"

PART V

Week 5: Argue No More! Setting the Plan in Motion

[Acknowledgments]

I wish to thank all those involved with this project at St. Martin's Press, especially my editor, Sheila Curry Oakes, for her insights and collaboration. Thanks also to my literary agent, Linda Roghaar, who recognized the need for this book and supported my ideas from the very beginning. Hats off as well to my professional colleagues and my own adult children from whom I have learned so much. And I would be remiss if I did not acknowledge all the parents and children I have worked with over the years for all their hard work and determination to make their family lives better and to raise children to become responsible, productive grown-ups.

The Brat Stops Here!

Real-Life Horror Stories
for Parents

SCENE 1: You're in Wal-Mart with your two children in tow, one walking alongside, the other seated in the cart. There is nothing unusual about this scene. Nor is it unusual when the older child takes off at a gallop for the toy section, utterly ignoring your plea for him to stop and come back. You go in pursuit at the same time your younger child decides she wants "out" of the cart, kicking and crying as she tries to squeeze out of the seat restraint. While you're trying to get to the runner and keep the climber seated, the tension builds and so does the drama. Your youngest is screaming and flailing her arms as you hold her shoulder with one hand to prevent her from falling as you attempt to steer your floppy-wheeled cart ever faster to catch up with your son. Finally you reach him only to see that he has pulled down an entire shelf of Legos onto himself, and is now also wailing and throwing his arms about.

All eyes are on you and your children. Several of the staring faces grimace with obvious disapproval. Embarrassed and angry, you stoop to clean up the Legos, imploring your son to help since he made the mess. He does nothing. Meanwhile, the little climber has been busy opening the seal on the lipstick you just picked out and is smearing it all over her hair and face with utter delight. Having cleaned up the Lego shelf as best you could, you grab your wandering son's wrist, vowing to not let go until you are through the check-out and out to the car. The little makeup artist has now broken off the lipstick—gone before you have even paid for it. Not surprisingly, the check-out lanes are long. Having run out of patience, as both children whine and cry, you feel like joining in. It takes everything you have to keep from shrieking out at the top of your lungs: *"Stop it!"*

SCENE 2: It is the first day at a new school for your six-year-old Sam, all dressed up in his new school clothes and so proud of his backpack. You wonder how he will fare when there are so many other kids who want the teacher's attention. You are excited for Sam and worried at the same time. He is such a bright child, but he has also had many scraps with other kids in kindergarten. At times he can be very sweet and will often sit for long periods of time paging through picture books. In those moments no one looking would ever expect that Sam was capable of exploding like a volcano. His eruptions are precisely why you were called to pick him up early from his previous school on several occasions. Sam's teacher had complained, "Once he goes off, there is no turning back, no matter what we do." Today will be nerve-wracking waiting to discover what he does.

The phone rings at 10:15. It is the school counselor asking you to come and retrieve Sam because he is "out of control." When you ask what happened, the counselor tells you: "The class was told to put away their artwork materials because it was story time. Sam was adamant about finishing his art project first. When his teacher came over and insisted he quit, Sam threw a tantrum, kicked his teacher's ankle, and ran to the corner of the room where he picked up the nearest book and flung it at the other children. He then firmly planted his feet, crossed his arms, and scowled at everyone. His teacher had to clear the room to get him to calm down. We simply cannot allow that kind of bad behavior here. Sam will be here in the school office with me until you come to get him."

SCENE 3: "Jenna, it's nearly time for us to go to your cousin's birthday party. Have you finished cleaning your room?"

[silence]

"Young lady, did you hear me?"

[silence]

"Jenna, I don't want to have to come up there!"

[silence]

Infuriated at being ignored, you pound your way upstairs only find Jenna playing a video game, lost in her own world. Though there is no doubt that she heard you, she does not respond. "Jenna!!" I am speaking to you! Put down that game and look at me!" Jenna slowly turns around and gives you a look that implies you are being a bother. "Jenna, you are nearly twelve years old. Why do I have to keep reminding you over and over to clean up your things? Put that video game down right now and get this done!"

"Why should I? It's my room. I can do whatever I want in here and it's none of your business. I like my room this way. Besides, I don't want to go to that stupid old birthday party anyway."

"You are going with us to your cousin's party, and that's that! If you don't start to listen to me and do what I say, there aren't going to be any video games or TV for you at all. Now get going! We are already late."

"That's not fair! This is *my* video game, and the TV is *our* family TV, not just yours. You are such a nag. And you're always picking on me. My friends' moms are nice, not like you! Their moms don't care if their rooms are a mess. You just like bossing me around. You're such a control freak! But you're *not* the boss of me!"

"Okay, that's it! I just can't stand this anymore! The rest of us are going to the party and you can just stay home, then! And don't think that you are going anywhere. You just stay right here in the house. I'll be calling every fifteen minutes to check up on you, so don't get any big ideas. We'll deal with this room business when I get home."

[The door slams; Jenna resumes her video game.]

Sound familiar? Unfortunately, scenes like these are not uncommon. Obnoxious behavior is making life miserable for so many parents. No parent wants to put up with children who become unmanageable tyrants. Despite our best efforts, tantrums, back talk, and disobedience continue because we don't know how else to handle these situations. Unfortunately, most of us get more training for driving than we do for parenting our children, so we don't know which way to turn to become an effective parent. Do we follow a traditional approach and do what our parents did? Do we just make it up as we go along? Or do we try plan after plan to the point where we are totally confused (as are our kids) and haven't made any positive changes in how we parent or in our kids' behavior?

No, to all of the above. It doesn't have to be that way. And it's not nearly so difficult to snuff out unwanted behaviors in your child as you have been led to believe. It honestly breaks my heart to see so many families struggling with willful children, especially when their parents are unknowingly fanning the flames with their reactions to their children's behavior. For many years I have helped parents apply my simple and highly effective "faucet approach" to stop tantrums, arguing, and obnoxiousness. In all but a handful of cases, no matter how severe the child's defiance, in just a few weeks these unwanted behaviors were significantly reduced. In many instances, the tantrums and disobedience have come to a screeching halt, and did not return. It is such a pleasure to see how much family members can enjoy each other and feel good about themselves when home is no longer a battlefield.

As chief psychologist for a large urban child guidance clinic and director of a suburban practice group, every day I have been dismayed by the number of children who are surly, demanding, out of control, and simply obnoxious. Their parents come to see me because they don't know what to do. They complain, "I just can't take it anymore! I have tried *everything*. Isn't there anything I can do to *stop it?*"

Unruly, smart-alecky children are not what parents ever dream of when they start a family. But as time goes by and parents struggle without success through a series of trial-and-error efforts to get rid of bad behavior, they become worn out and hopeless. Sadly, many of them ultimately give in and give up in utter defeat.

When parents' dreams of a calm, loving, and fun family seem out of reach, they don't know where to turn. Advice from other family members and friends has not helped. Piles of parenting magazines and books may have been of little use as well. Bookstore shelves are overflowing with as many parenting guides as there are diet books. Undoubtedly there are some valuable lessons and useful ideas in these books, but I find that too many of them complicate the matter by searching for some deep reason why this bad behavior exists. In my view, when it comes to raising kids, the hunt for deep-seated, underlying causes is generally a waste of time. The source of bad behavior is rarely a mystery—that's the first piece of good news—because it's nearly always a mix of a child's difficult temperament and misguided parenting methods. The second piece of good news is that the fix is no longer a mystery either.

I would go so far as to say that at least 50 percent of the child behavior problems that are referred to mental health clinics for medication could have been remedied without medication. There are legitimate reasons for medicating certain children, but that is rarely the first and best choice. Yet one can see how easy it would be to think that is the only remaining alternative when parents believe behavioral approaches won't work. Choosing medication first is a very understandable response, but also a tragic one, because I have an approach that I know from years of experience really works. I have used it effectively with many types of families from many cultural and social backgrounds and with children others have considered incorrigible. When parents follow the *Dr. J Way*, it works!

With the *Dr. J Way*, there is no need to interpret each incident of misbehavior as a different problem requiring a new response from you. Parents who have used my method are amazed by its simplicity, because they have felt stumped and tried so many things to change their child's behavior that they assumed the solution would be especially complicated. Not so.

In these pages we will quickly get right down to the specific dos and don'ts of my program. You will not need to plow through hundreds of dry child psychology pages that go into excruciating detail to explain why your child doesn't behave. You will be provided with real-world examples drawn from my experiences with families (names and identifying information have been changed to protect their privacy), and a few words about difficult temperaments. Then you will be instructed step by step to create a personalized behavior plan for you, your child, and your family that you will put into effect in no time at all. It will be the end of nagging, arguing, reminding, lecturing, threatening, fighting, yelling, or exacting physical punishment. Besides, these responses to misbehavior are ineffective and most of the time they only serve to make matters worse.

To change your child's behavior, consistency is the key,

which is why an efficient, easy-to-follow approach that applies to nearly every situation is a must. Of course, there may be a few exceptions, but probably far fewer than you think. And, because the approach is so clear-cut, everyone involved—parents, grandparents, babysitters, teachers—will know exactly what to do and what not to do. If the parents I work with whose kids display the most serious of challenges (e.g., hitting siblings, kicking teachers, throwing rocks at cars, destroying property, spitting at kids on the bus, getting so out of control at school that the police have to intervene) can make their children behave, so can you. This approach works for kids with all kinds of temperaments, from easygoing to high-strung, and who have all levels of behavior problems. Some are fairly co-operative youngsters who only fail to turn in their homework or skip out on clearing the table after dinner. At the other extreme, I have helped parents whose children have gone so far as to threaten to run away or kill themselves if parents refuse to buy them a video game or didn't allow the child to attend a rock concert. To the amazement of these parents, in just a few weeks the most radical of their children's behaviors were extinguished.

Better yet, the *Dr. J Way* allows you to do more than guide your child to better behavior. It can also increase your child's patience, willingness to compromise, self-control, acceptance of responsibility, and self-esteem, all of which are essential for healthy development. Your job as parents is to prepare your child to become a responsible adult. This book can help you do just that. No matter how much of a handful your child has been, and no matter how skeptical you are about making changes, the one thing I know for sure is that if you keep doing what you've been doing, you will continue to get the same results—negative behavior from your child.

If you change what you've been doing you'll have no more tantrums, arguing, or bad behavior in just a few weeks. In less than two months your family could be living much more happily in a battle-free zone. What a pleasure to rediscover the joy in parenting when play, laughter, sharing, and loving moments with your child overshadow disagreements and upsets. You have little to lose and everything to gain. You can start by making a step-by-step plan for *you* and *your child* that will change your family life in *five weeks or less!*

—*Dr. Mary-Elaine Jacobsen*

[Part I]

WEEK 1

Understanding Temperament
and Bad Behavior

[1]

What's Wrong? Why Won't My Child Behave?

O ver the years I have worked with hundreds of exasperated parents who struggle with children who will not behave. They all share five things:

1. They did not set out to raise a stubbornly disobedient or obnoxious child, and they don't know what's wrong.

2. They are consistently inconsistent—trapped in a loop of trial-and-error attempts to get their children to stop behaving badly and do what they are told without endless arguing and nagging.

3. They simultaneously feel like failures and victims when they see other children who are pleasant and well behaved.

4. They are extremely disheartened because they have tried everything they can think of to get their child to behave, with little or no success.

5. They have come to believe that the cause of their child's misbehavior is deep-seated and complicated, and that it will take a near miracle to make things better.

When desperate parents ask me, "Why won't my child behave?" I tell them, "Several things may be contributing to your child's noncompliance and misbehavior. It is likely that you have a 'difficult temperament' child. Each of us has a temperament (disposition, character, spirit) that is present from birth and is strongly influenced by genetics. As we grow our temperaments are shaped by our environments and experiences, and they also affect the way we relate to others and they relate to us."

Very early in life, children with difficult temperaments show signs of future distress. They may exhibit irregular patterns of sleeping, eating, or elimination. Many are hard-to-manage infants who are colicky, irritable, and not easily calmed. Children with difficult temperaments may have trouble adjusting to changes (e.g., new foods, people around them, places, or schedules). If overstimulated they may put on loud displays of resistance and are sometimes aggressive. Oftentimes they have high activity levels, are fidgety, restless, and "into everything." Many highly sensitive children are easily bothered by itchy fabrics, bright lights, loud music, alarm clocks, or school bells. Some of these children struggle with sensory integration deficits and may benefit from occupational therapy. Some have trouble with structure and routine, seeming to prefer it when things don't go according to plan. Whether they are basically oversensitive or have sensory integration problems, it is easy to see how this temperamental style can wreak havoc with classroom expectations and family routines.

Being easily bothered can also be related to high levels of distractibility. Highly distractible children notice and pay attention to nearly everything going on around them *and* within themselves (ideas, fantasies, hunger, and so on). Inadequate persistence is another common trait of difficult-temperament children, which typically causes problems at home and at school—they become disproportionately irritated or annoyed when things don't go smoothly, or when they are interrupted. Although all children present a variety of emotional reactions, these children are inclined to be negative more often than not. Typically they are "hot reactors" whose intense emotional responses often exhaust their parents and teachers. Observers of these children describe them as demanding, pushy, oppositional, and capable of flying sky-high into explosive tantrums with little provocation.

Knowing whether or not your child has a difficult temperament is not meant to label any child in a negative way and set them up for a self-fulfilling prophecy. Rather, the purpose of identifying temperamental traits in children is twofold: (a) to stop blaming the child for something that is inborn, and (b) to help parents get a better idea of how to raise their children successfully. Experts in child behavior have identified the temperamental traits listed in the chart on page 17 as "difficult." You can use this chart to get a rough idea of how easy or difficult it may be to raise your child. Think in terms of your child's developmental history overall, recalling how he or she was as an infant and during early childhood as well as now.

Of course, there are many combinations of these temperamental styles and they may be expressed in varying degrees from mild to moderate to extreme. Yet even children with extremely difficult temperaments can be helped to manage their temperamental tendencies in ways that are more effective and acceptable. Difficult-temperament children are hard to understand and manage because their temperament influences how everyone relates to them. When their inborn tendencies and behavioral habits collide with family, peer, or school expectations, watch out! Some useful tips on managing problematic temperament types are included in Appendix A, page 181.

Understanding a child's temperament and accepting the fact that the difficult-temperament styles listed are largely inborn helps parents get out of the blame game, past the all the "whys," and onto how to fix what needs fixing, with parenting strategies that really work. Any fix is not the right fix. A bad-fit response to a difficult-temperament child is like pouring gas on a fire. That is why it is so important to fully understand the effect of what *you* say, do, and don't do in response to your child, because your choices will either make things better or worse.

If you are fed up like so many of the parents who come to see me as a last-ditch effort, and if like them you feel like you

IDENTIFYING DIFFICULT TEMPERAMENT	
ACTIVITY LEVEL—*How active is your child in general?*	Highly Active
ADAPTABILITY—*How easily does your child deal with transitions and changes or shift from one activity to another?*	Slow to Adapt
APPROACH/WITHDRAW—*How does your child typically respond to new situations or new people?*	Withdraws
DISTRACTIBILITY—*How often does your child's attention get sidetracked by unimportant things and/or is off-task?*	Highly Distractible
INTENSITY—*How much energy and emotion does your child put into his or her reactions (e.g., either loves or hates things; laughs or cries loudly and dramatically)?*	Intense Responses
MOOD—*Does your child seem to naturally react to the world in a primarily positive or negative way?*	Negative Mood
PERSISTENCE—*How well can your child stick with a task despite interruptions or frustrations?*	Low Persistence
REGULARITY—*How predictable or consistent are your child's habits and daily routines, including biological patterns (e.g., waking, appetite, tired at night)? How comfortable is your child with structure and schedules?*	Low Regularity
SENSORY THRESHOLD—*How sensitive is your child to touch, taste, aromas, light, sound? How easily bothered is your child by changes in the environment?*	High Sensitivity

have already tried everything, it may seem nearly impossible to get your hopes up about changing your child's behavior. The truth of the matter is that at this point you have nothing to lose and everything to gain. We already know if you keep doing what you're doing, you will certainly keep getting what you're getting. So, try very hard to imagine what it will feel like when you know exactly when to ignore what your child is doing, what to do, what to say, and why you should do it that way. Needless to say, this does not mean that your child's naturally difficult temperament will disappear. It *does* mean that your response to unwanted behaviors can and will make a real and positive difference.

Bearing that in mind, picture yourself as calm, intelligent, and sure when your child totally ignores your instructions or flies into a kicking, screaming rage, thrashing about like cars in the smash-up derby. See yourself as a confident parent who knows precisely how to react. Then, create an image of your child calming down and learning to obey you, and following the rules. This is the vision to hang on to over the coming weeks. This image has become reality for the vast majority of parents I have worked with who held out little or no hope that their child would ever behave. By following the plan for a few weeks these parents were overjoyed to see their dreams of a peaceful and happier family come true. If they could do it, so can you.

Fitting Temperament with Parenting Style

Child development researchers have examined various qualities most parents would like to see in their children, such as independence, self-reliance, curiosity, friendliness, self-control, and a desire to achieve. These researchers have also interviewed parents in an effort to determine parenting styles, and were especially interested in finding out which parenting characteristics contributed to the development of the desired qualities in children. Evaluating parenting style revolves around two key elements: parental response (including characteristics such as the parent's degree of warmth, acceptance, and supportiveness, and involvement), and parental control (including such things as a parent's willingness to set and maintain rules, confronting children when they misbehave, fairness, and tolerance). Based on the researchers' investigations of how parents used their authority, four fundamental parenting styles emerged:

1. **Balanced: High Love/High Limits**—These parents operate on basic principles of democracy. Democratic equality takes into account each family member's personal worth, value, and dignity. Equality does *not* mean equally in charge or imply equal votes for parents and children. Parents retain veto power over decisions that affect their children and the well-being of the family. Their children know they are loved and that their parents expect them to follow certain standards and

do their fair share. Parents who balance love and limits respond affectionately to their children and set firm and clearcut rules that build trust as well as good behavior. They are respectfully and calmly assertive. They do not argue, shame, nag, cajole, threaten, hit, yell, or tolerate bad behavior. They use more effective parenting methods that are firm and supportive versus punitive, and offer their children reasonable, progressive challenges while permitting them to develop at their own pace. These evenhanded parents model social responsibility, self-regulation, and cooperation, and show by their decisions and actions the difference between right and wrong. Balanced parents recognize that consequences and occasional frustrations are reasonable and normal experiences for their children. Their underlying objective is to encourage their children to develop independence and responsibility. The purpose of any disciplinary action is to guide and teach, not to punish or control. They help their children learn to be self-reliant and to solve problems.

Children of parents who balance love and limits typically feel secure and accepted. They experience an emerging sense of strength as they conquer difficulties and find satisfaction in both achievement and contribution, and they learn to accept responsibility. They make wise choices, cope with setbacks, monitor themselves, and make changes for the better, and are better equipped to succeed in a workforce that relies on cooperative problem-solving. They are usually friendly, cooperative, confident, and not afraid to try new things or take reasonable risks. They can be flexible, adaptable, and sensitive to the wishes and needs of others. Just as their parents presented a model of balance, when these children grow up they will be able to balance external demands for conformity with their needs for individuality and independence.

2. Indulgent: High Love/Low Limits—These parents make very few demands on their children because they fear confrontations and may also believe rules, structure, and behavioral expectations may stifle their child's creativity or "natural self." They often think that love and limit-setting are incompatible. Consequently, these permissive parents spend a lot of time with the child communicating, negotiating, and reasoning, and trying to make their child feel special. They are warm, accepting, and encouraging and do indeed provide their children with much love, but they are also at risk of becoming enmeshed with them. These parents tolerate bad behavior or dismiss it as innocuous, they rarely take a stand that will make their child unhappy, and often overprotect their child from any type of criticism.

Researchers have found that children of permissive parents have poor self-control, are impulsive, immature, and do not take responsibility for their own choices and actions. These children often suffer from self-esteem taken too far and see themselves as entitled to whatever they want and at liberty to do whatever they please. Although these children usually have adequate social skills and lower levels of depression, they are more likely to perform poorly in their academic work and to develop problems such as self-centeredness, arguing with teachers, truancy, shoplifting, and disrespect for rules and authority.

3. Punitive: Low Love/High Limits—These parents are strict, often rigid, and demand unquestioning obedience because they consider it a virtue. They rely on punishment as their primary way of making their children submit to their directives. There is little give-and-take between parent and child. These parents consider limits to be more important than love, and they confuse healthy discipline with punishment. They use external discipline tactics and are swift to respond harshly to any sign of disrespect.

It appears as though harsh punishment is effective because when the external threat or force is great enough the child may indeed obey. However, when the threat or force is removed, these children revolt and act out in an effort to pay back their parents for being punished. Worse yet, they often fail to develop any internal sense of right and wrong. Children of harsh, punitive parents are also quick to react and be intolerant of others. Most of them do not feel close to their parents, and many of them fear their parents. They become followers who rarely take the initiative, lack adequate social skills, are not very eager to learn new things, and are low in creative spontaneity. Although many of these children perform adequately in school, they tend to be uninterested and under-involved, have low self-esteem, and have higher levels of depression.

4. Uninvolved: Low Love/Low Limits—These parents demand little from their children and pay little positive attention to them. They also seldom respond to their children with warmth, affection, or acceptance, and primarily keep their distance and remain on the periphery of their child's life. They show little interest in their children and often treat them as if they are a bother, encouraging them to watch TV, to go outside, or to occupy themselves in their rooms because the parents are "busy." Some of these parents are so tied up in their careers or other activities that there is virtually no time left over for parental involvement. Detached parents overlook opportunities to guide their child and shape their behavior. When they do try to discipline their children they often get caught up in vicious power struggles that end either in them giving up and giving in, or becoming abusive. In the worst cases their children are frequently rejected or seriously neglected. In many respects these children are left to raise themselves without proper guidance and supervision. These children generally have the most difficulties as they grow up and perform the most poorly in all domains.

The *Dr. J Way* parenting method advocates the first of these four styles—Balanced: High Love/High Limits— because it has been shown to be the best choice overall for raising healthy, competent, responsible young people, which is the primary job of every parent. While changing the way you've been doing things may be challenging, all the steps will be laid out plainly and you will ultimately realize that the method is not complicated and can be incorporated into any family situation.

As we go forward, keep these things in mind: Temperament may be built in, but it is not your child's destiny carved in stone. A good fit between parenting and childhood learning experiences can do a lot to influence behavior and encourage responsibility. Parents who are tuned in to their child's temperamental style and also recognize that their child has particular strengths are far better prepared to help their children grow up well. Once parents understand what makes their child tick and apply a consistent, research-based, brain-based behavior plan such as this one, even high-strung children can learn how to modulate their responses and find new ways to manage themselves so things at home and school are less troublesome. You can rely on this plan to work where others have not because it is founded on a combination of child brain development and proven behavior management strategies.

Although you will need to understand a little about why your child behaves "like that," you do not need to read hundreds of dry pages about child development and behavioral psychology. And you do not need to learn dozens of complicated ways to handle your child's various behavior problems. One of the greatest benefits of this plan is that it is straightforward and to the point. The end of arguing, reminding, pleading, lecturing, and nagging is just around the corner! There is no need to make things up as you go—you will know in advance exactly what to say and do no matter what your child tries next. Once you get the *Dr. J Way* you will have a portable plan that is ready to go and will fit nearly every situation. At least you will be in charge and effective as a parent, and everyone will win.

[2]

Jack the Brat and
Jill the Pill in Real Life

No parent wants to think of his or her child as a "brat" or "pill," and of course we never want to call a child names that imply they are bad through and through. The title of this book includes the word "brat" because, like it or not, when other people encounter children who behave badly, that is often what they are thinking. We want to stop the "brat behaviors" here and now—that is our primary goal. Yet even if a child behaves like the proverbial brat or pill, it is always important to separate our spoken comments about bad behavior from suggestions that the child is fundamentally bad. For instance, when a child misbehaves it is essential that we point out the unwanted act: "Hitting your sister is unacceptable, Jack," vs. attacking the actor: "Stop it, Jack! You are such a bad boy!"

As we have seen, children who are cantankerous and cause

trouble for those around them probably inherited some unfortunate temperamental traits. While a difficult temperament is not a license for bad behavior, neither does it render the child bad through and through. When you take a look at these children with a compassionate and understanding eye, under the disagreeable surface you can catch a glimpse of a "good kid" whose behavior is bad because he or she is caught up in a drama of opposition, conflict, and overreaction. Seeing the good child is critical if change is to occur, because when parents throw their hands up in the air and believe that they are powerless and therefore destined to live in misery every day, they usually get what they expect.

We must also acknowledge the fact that children are not raised in a vacuum. Battlefield dramas are kept alive, at least in part, because of how parents, teachers, and others around these children respond to them. Understanding how difficult temperament and bad-fit responses conspire to create horror stories for parents is perhaps best explained with the following examples. Although not exhaustive by any means, this cast of characters is typical of the problem children my clients struggle with day in and day out.

The Aggressive Child: *"No Fair! Now You're Going to Get It!"*

Studies indicate that somewhere between 11 and 14 million children in this country have serious emotional and behavioral problems. The vast majority of these children are easily angered, do not try to control their anger, and act out aggressively toward property and other people. Their M.O. for dealing with frustration is hostility. They instill much of their interpersonal relationships with a degree of animosity that far exceeds reason. It is typical for them to misinterpret social situations. And when they misread what others say and do, they retaliate as though the other person is malicious and out to get them, and the resulting aggression is based in a self-righteous belief that revenge is a suitable response and the other person deserves it. For example, ten-year-old Reggie was known by everyone at school as a hothead, and most of the other kids steered clear whenever he was in sight. One afternoon as he walked down the busy hall another child inadvertently bumped into him, knocking Reggie's books to the floor. Although it was clearly an accident and the other boy was about to help him pick up the books, Reggie immediately interpreted the mishap as a personal attack and exploded, hitting the boy over the head with a notebook until a teacher hauled him off to the principal's office, where he was promptly suspended from school for three days. "Hey! Let go of me! I didn't do anything, he started it!" Reggie cried.

Habitual, angry lashing out creates an environment of chronic tension and unease. When the angry child explodes, the vented anger only ignites a bigger fire, which in turn he justifies as his right to be angry. This vicious cycle stems from a rigid set of internal "shoulds" that the child applies to others without any room for error (e.g., everyone *should* do what I want; I *should* always go first; you *should* not apply your rules to me; I *should* get my way). They cannot put themselves in other people's shoes and have not learned to take responsibility for their own actions. Some of these children hold their anger and resentment inside like a volcano. Their injured-party self-talk convinces them that they have been done terrible wrongs and someone should pay. The least thing can set off the volcano at any time, so you never know when fireballs will start to fly.

Shaina was a twelve-year-old girl whose parents were unwittingly contributing to her antisocial ways. Because they lacked effective discipline skills and often relied on manipulation or bribing to get Shaina to do what they asked, she learned to be coercive also. Shaina and her parents engaged in a tug-of-war that was fueled by hostile talk, threats, and aggression. When Shaina's arguing and defiance went on and on, her father, having reached his limits, grabbed her arm forcefully, and physically threatened her, roaring, "I am your father and you will do as I say or you'll regret it! Mark my words. Now get in there and do those dishes and I don't want to hear another word out of you all night! Do I make myself clear?!"

There was no doubt in Shaina's mind that her father was the dominant member of the family and that he was indeed a threat. Living in an atmosphere of threat filled her with unresolved feelings of helplessness and injustice, which set her up to retaliate in any way she could, including argument, noncompliance, a snotty attitude, and her own threats and aggression toward her younger brother. She slammed doors, took a hammer to her brother's bike, tore up one of her mother's favorite blouses, and kicked the cat when no one was looking. Anyone who knew her recognized the big chip she carried on her shoulder wherever she went, and most people steered clear. Her tough act and attempts to intimidate others gave her a sense of power and superiority. No one was going to see her as weak, including her teachers or anyone else who got in her face.

Impulsive by nature, during the last week of the school year Shaina was feeling even more audacious than usual. When her teacher asked her to help Jessie, a fellow student, pack away textbooks for the summer, she felt persecuted: "Why me? I don't see you asking Tressa or LeeAnne to do it. Besides, you're not the boss of me! If you want those books packed, do it yourself, or get some other flunky like that stupid Jessie to do it for you." Naturally Shaina's behavior pushed the teacher to take the upper hand, and the conflict escalated. As her teacher approached, wagging her index finger, Shaina lost her cool. The class watched in horror as Shaina slapped the teacher's hand away and threatened, "There's more where that came from if you don't back off, lady!" Within a half hour Shaina was being carted off in cuffs, screaming in the arms of the police that she was being harassed. Shaina's parents were referred to me by a social worker at the juvenile justice system where Shaina was sent for ten days. Her parents blamed the teacher and "those out-of-line cops" and Shaina blamed them all.

This was not an easy case because it was clear to me that the entire pattern of family dynamics would have to change. Fortunately, the juvenile detention center incident had really shaken everyone in the family, especially Shaina. We put together a set of behavioral expectations for all the members of the family, including Shaina's younger sister, who was also beginning to throw some pretty nasty tantrums. All the expectations fit with the *Dr. J Way* program.

The Center-of-the-Universe Child: *"Me, Me, Me"*

It is normal for children to want things and ask for them, and not always politely. At certain developmental stages—two years and again in adolescence—most children go through periods when they consider themselves deprived and demand that their needs be met immediately. Center-of-the-universe children, however, are consistently unsatisfied and insistent. According to them, they "need" something nearly all the time. A trip to any discount or grocery store will give you some real-life cases in point.

These children develop the art of whining, nagging, and placing themselves at center stage on Academy Award–winning levels. They feel entitled and portray the "you owe me" role all the time. These children yank their parents' shirt sleeves relentlessly, despite the fact that Mom or Dad is talking on the phone. They interrupt and intrude on people and boss other kids around like little dictators. Their primary weapons are badgering and guilt induction: "Mom! Maaaahhmmmm!!! I want _____ now!!! Pleeeeeezze, *Mom*!!! Give me _____! You said I could!!! That's not fair!!! You're mean. I want a different mom who's nice!! Whaaaah!" The message this child repeatedly sends is this: "I deserve to be the center of attention because I am special and I deserve to have you drop everything for me right now, and if you don't do what I want I am going to make you miserable."

If the child's behavior and demandingness is not put in check it will only get worse. Children do not automatically outgrow acting this way. If you are ever within earshot of a raging executive who, amidst foul language, sends everything flying off his desk in one brutish sweep, you are seeing the adult version of the center-of-the-universe child.

While some of the roots of self-centeredness may lie in a difficult temperament, much of it is learned. The child who is doted on and indulged cannot view things from any other perspective than that of his or her own. These children do not display empathy for others or recognize that other people have needs and wishes, too. They are so used to focusing on themselves and getting their way that when they don't they think, "If I don't get my way I have the right to blow up." These children are also blamers. Whatever goes against their wishes and however they behave badly in response, it's always someone else's fault: "She made me hit her. She wouldn't give me that toy and I want it!" When it comes to ducking responsibility, these children can outshine the best spin doctors in Washington, D.C. Entitled children erroneously link gratification with feeling loved, which is the basis for trying to instill guilt in their parents: "If you don't give me what I want you don't love me." They also convey a second hidden message—"If you don't do what I want I won't love you anymore"—that can really tug at the heartstrings of parents who are unaware that they are being bamboozled by a manipulative youngster.

Tonya was indeed one of these difficult children who saw herself as the shining and rightful center of the universe. Her mother, Janell, was a single parent who had no idea what to do with Tonya, who could nag her to the point of utter exhaustion. Not only had Tonya learned by experience to pressure her mother relentlessly until she got satisfaction, by the time Tonya was nine Janell was programmed to give in because it was the only way she knew to stop the pestering for a few moments of peace and quiet. It was a predictable cause-and-effect operation. From time to time Janell would try to put her foot down, but Tonya would only react more strongly and act out more aggressively. Pretty soon Janell was walking on eggshells trying to anticipate Tonya's every wish, to avoid an explosion.

Because Tonya was so successful with her parental bullying tactics, she engaged in similar behavior with others. At a springtime outdoor birthday party for Keisha, one of Tonya's fourth-grade classmates, Tonya put on a display that for all purposes ruined the party for everyone. The stage was set from the get-go, since the party wasn't for or about Tonya. Tonya was annoyed by the attention Keisha was receiving from everyone from the minute the party began, so she moved in to take over the center. "My birthday is coming up next month," Tonya ragged, "and *I'm* going to have the biggest cake and best party ever. Just wait and see. And my mom will get me anything I want." Oblivious to the eye-rolling from the other guests, Tonya set out to win every game they played. When she and her partner lost the wheelbarrow race Tonya blew: "You stupid idiot! How could you be so slow? We could have won, but you didn't even try!" after which she trudged inside in a huff without looking back. Having witnessed this outburst, Keisha's mother approached Tonya gingerly and asked her to apologize. That was the last straw for Tonya. "Why should I? It was her fault! I didn't want to come to this stupid party anyway! I'm taking my present and going home—call my mother right now!" Janell found her daughter sitting on Keisha's doorstep enraged at what had happened to *her*, and drove home feeling totally frustrated, embarrassed, and powerless as Tonya ranted on and on.

I worked with Tonya and Janell during the weeks that followed. At first Janell was doubtful that anything she might do differently could have any effect on Tonya's obnoxiousness. We agreed that Tonya would have to be well-versed in the *Dr. J Way* plan, and that we would even practice some predictable situations using role play. When Janell felt confident that she was prepared, she asked her own mother to join us for two sessions to bring her up to speed with the program so that Janell could take a break on the weekends and Tonya's grandmother could carry out the plan without missing a beat. This ensured the consistency that was going to be a critical factor in the outcome. Tonya was present at the next session so her mom could explain the expectations and how privileges would work, with everyone hearing it the same way. It was obvious that Tonya was furious about the plan and tried to sabotage it several times: "This is stupid! I'm not going to do it and that's just too bad for you! Besides, you can't take away my privileges! You have no right!" As expected, Tonya stormed from my office in a flurry of drama. She soon learned that her mother and grandmother now knew that histrionics were nothing more than coercion tactics and that ignoring was their new response. When things at home calmed down in a few weeks and Tonya was no longer nagging and was even offering to help her mom and grandmother, I suggested she join a girls' social skills group to learn better ways to deal with peers and to practice sharing, taking turns, and letting others be in charge. By the time she entered the fifth grade Tonya's behavior had made a 180-degree turnaround. The students who knew her were astonished at the difference, and within just a few weeks she had new friends and was a much happier child. Needless to say, Janell was thrilled with the change. To be sure, she and Tonya still tangled from time to time, but only rarely and very briefly, because Janell was able to step away from the urge to argue within seconds.

The Defiant Child: *"I Won't, and You Can't Make Me!"*

If there was a contest for ignoring grown-ups, eight-year-old Anthony was sure to win. At ten he had been developing his "take no notice" skills for years. He vacillated between giving his parents the brush-off and unconditional refusal. His father, Carlos, sarcastically complained, "That boy doesn't hear anything I say and has a one-word vocabulary of *no*!" By the time they came to see me, Anthony and his parents were experts at the "you can't make me" tango. And the older Anthony became, the less likely it was that his parents could get him to do anything without a battle. This was all quite evident every morning, so much so that Carlos had taken to leaving an hour early for work just to escape the inevitable skirmishes, hoping Maria, Anthony's mom, would make it through somehow:

MARIA: "Anthony, your alarm has been ringing for ten minutes. Get out of bed or you'll miss the school bus." Five minutes later: "Anthony! Do you hear me? Get up and get going right now, young man!"

ANTHONY: "*Mom*!! Shut up! Stop nagging me! I'll get up when I'm ready to get up, and not before! So get off my back!"

Fifteen minutes later Anthony moseys into the kitchen with the scowl on his face so nasty it could put the lights out. Maria: "Well, it's about time. You have three minutes to brush your teeth and get out to the corner. If you would just get up on time you wouldn't have to be rushed like this. It's driving me crazy!"

Anthony responds by going even slower. "If you weren't such a nag maybe I would get up sooner. And so what if I miss the bus? Big deal, you've got a car for a reason, you know. Just stuff a rag in it and get your car keys. Hurry up, Mom! I'm gonna be late, and it's all your fault."

Similar scenes occurred every day after school whenever it was time to turn off the TV and do homework, finish chores, get ready for bed, turn out the lights, and so forth. For the most part, Anthony did exactly as he pleased, was virtually no help around the house, and felt completely put out if someone so much as asked him to lift a finger or interrupt what he was doing. Without intervention, the situation in Anthony's home was not going to be a pretty sight when he reached age sixteen. To make matters worse, his two younger brothers were starting to copy his back talk and insolent ways, which was making home life a nightmare for Maria and Carlos.

After our first meeting, where I witnessed Anthony's rudeness firsthand, I invited Carlos and Maria to come in without Anthony or his brothers. They needed to hear how I could help them regain control and put a stop to all the power struggles without the boys arguing and interrupting us. Their faces began to brighten as I described similar cases where parents at their wits' end had successfully turned their children's behavior around. And when I painted a vivid picture of Anthony as a big, mouthy, defiant teenager if they didn't act soon, they were quickly on board with the program. We developed the plan together and included age-appropriate rules, expectations, and consequences for all three boys and for Maria and Carlos as well. Because Carlos traveled a fair amount for his job and we knew that Anthony tended to behave better when another adult was present, Maria engaged the help of a close friend who lived nearby. It was very likely that the first few days of the plan would be difficult because Anthony was not the type to give up his power-struggle habits easily. In situations where Maria felt she needed some support to hold her ground, her friend came to the house. Anthony was less willing to lose total control in front of someone else, and Maria was able to successfully ignore his whining and badgering. After a few weeks of Anthony's failure to coerce his parents back into the battle zone, he settled down and became quite compliant. He had learned to stop nagging and badgering, because it just didn't work anymore. He also learned that he had a great number of privileges that he enjoyed, and that when his privileges were revoked the only person who had caused that to happen was the one he saw in the mirror.

The Demanding Child: *"I Want What I Want When I Want It!"*

Kevin was seven, and the long-awaited only child of Robb and Alicia. They had dreamed of being parents for many years and were thrilled when Kevin arrived. From day one they wanted only the best for their beloved son. When Kevin cried they responded appropriately with food, a change of diaper, or comfort. Without a doubt they were loving, caring parents, despite the fact that Kevin would be considered a difficult temperament child—colicky, fussy, easily upset, and very hard to calm. So it was quite understandable that his parents became used to responding immediately to his pleas for satisfaction. But as time went by this went too far, and as Kevin outgrew infancy Robb and Alicia continued to jump to meet Kevin's every demand. Little by little they began to realize they had lost control and Kevin was running the show. By the time he was five he could have been the poster boy for instant gratification. The minute he looked annoyed or perturbed his loving parents took note and flew into action. Their favorite response to Kevin's pouting was a highly concerned, "What's wrong, Kevin?" The more he fussed and fretted, the more Robb and Alicia paid attention to Kevin's wants and wishes as if each one of them was an actual need. At every turn they tried to predict Kevin's desires, believing that if his "needs" were anticipated and immediately satisfied, all would be well. And so it was, at least for the few minutes until he wanted something else.

Unintentionally, Kevin was being trained to have no tolerance for frustration, little ability to overcome obstacles on his own, no capacity to allow his "needs" to linger unmet for any amount of time, and to throw a fit to punish anyone around him who did not anticipate and indulge his every wish. He learned by experience that (a) he needed only to hang out his lower lip to command attention and service, (b) he should expect to be attended to whenever things weren't just so, and (c) lack of immediate response by parents deserved to be punished via a swift and obnoxious tantrum.

Kevin's parents were not the only ones who had trouble with him. Other kids in the neighborhood tended to play with Kevin once, and that was enough. Sharing and taking turns were not on his to-do list. Even Kevin's grandparents began to make excuses about having him spend time at their house. Robb and Alicia were beside themselves when Kevin was suspended from school four times while still in kindergarten and five times in first grade before being asked to go to another school. Second grade wasn't going much better. Robb and Alicia were at their wits' end.

When Robb and Alicia brought Kevin in for an assessment I took a complete history and also observed the interactions between Kevin and his parents. I then asked Robb and Alicia to wait in the lobby while I met with Kevin alone. Not unexpectedly, Kevin sat across from me with a surly expression and his arms folded, silently declaring he would not cooperate, no matter what. I gave him three choices of what we could do together: draw, read a story, or put together a puzzle. Not being used to limited choices Kevin asserted himself by standing up and pointing out a game on a high shelf, stomping his feet, and shouting between clenched teeth, "No! I want to play that!" I then calmly repeated the three choices one more time. At this point Kevin upped the ante shouting, "I said, I want to play that—now get it down!!" I turned back to my desk and began to do paperwork without saying a word. Mystified, Kevin started to bang on the chair, to stomp his feet louder, and to fling a nearby toy Frisbee-style as hard as he could against the door, immediately after which he ran to the corner, folded his arms in defiance, and yelled, "I hate you!" After a few minutes, without turning around, I calmly said, "That doesn't work in here, Kevin. But you may stand there as long as you like. When you decide to pick up the book and put it back nicely we can go find your parents."

The next several minutes were fraught with sighs of disgust, throat clearing, muttering nasty comments, and foot stomping. Kevin stood his ground, but to no avail. Ultimately he tired of this battle of the wills, shuffled loudly over to where the book lay, picked it up, and placed it not so gently on the table, after which I said, "That's much better, Kevin. I knew you could do it." The cheeky, I-hate-your-guts look on his face had been replaced with a look of calm bewilderment. It was obvious that Kevin had behaved this way before to different results. It didn't work this time. As Kevin and I began to walk down the hall toward his parents, the drama began anew, just as I expected. As soon as Kevin was within eyesight of his parents he ran toward them, crying and waving his arms wildly. He pointed an accusing finger at me and put on his "victim" face. Just as Kevin had come to expect, his parents grabbed at the bait, hugged him up, and scowled at me, barking, "What did you do?" They failed to notice the smirk on little Kevin's victorious face. Clearly we had a lot of work ahead of us, and fortunately, when I diagrammed the chain of events to Robb and Alicia and explained how they were playing into Kevin's difficult temperament, they began to see the light and we went forward from there.

I laid out the *Dr. J Way* program for them in detail, carefully explaining that they needed to be in agreement with each other, fully prepared, and determined to stick with it for the next few weeks. We explored what things might occur that would tempt them to give in and planned for how they could work together as a team to prevent that. We met again once a week and I provided some phone encouragement in between sessions. At the end of the five weeks Robb and Alicia came in for their last visit. From the look of utter relief and delight on their faces I could tell they had been successful with Kevin: "We are *so* amazed at the difference in Kevin! We actually love being home with him now, and we can take him places without being on pins and needles all the time. His grandparents think a miracle has happened. And not one complaint from school in the past three weeks—a new record for Kevin. We always knew he wasn't really a bad kid, but until now we just didn't know how to manage him. What a relief!"

The Spectator-Sport Child: *"Nooooo! You're Stupid and I Hate You!"*

One of my favorite stories about public displays of obnoxiousness involves six-year-old Jeb and his father, Matt. Jeb had originally been very close to his dad, but when his parents divorced a year earlier Jeb blamed his father and never seemed to be able to let go of his anger about it. He knew just where his father's hot buttons were and precisely when to push them. He primed the pump every time he came to spend the weekend with his father by complaining how he never gets to have any fun when he is there, and that he wished he could just stay at home with his mom and new stepfather, though in truth he didn't much care for the man. Nonetheless, it put Matt on the defensive and he felt pressured to compete with the new stepfather for Jeb's respect and affection. Although on some level Matt recognized that his son was taking advantage of the situation, he wasn't sure how to respond. He alternated between being overly strict and overly submissive.

Jeb was a clever boy with an axe to grind. He would wait for the opportune moment to mortify his father in public. It was Jeb's way of throwing down the gauntlet and daring his father to take him on. His mother had learned that it was best to ignore Jeb's temper tantrums. Regrettably, Matt paid them a great deal of attention, especially when they were out together in public. When they were at the ball game and Jeb didn't like the ice-cream cone his father bought for him, he launched it over the heads of the poor fans unfortunate enough to sit in front of them. Jeb enjoyed every minute watching his father apologize for the mess, trying in vain to wipe down their shirts or offer them money for dry cleaning. Church was another prime target area. Despite Matt's pleas for Jeb to be respectful "for just one hour," prayer time was Jeb's invitation to kick the pew, giggle uncontrollably, or make fart noises with the back of his hand. And what did that get him? In response to his behavior he got a quick ticket out of church through a bevy of disapproving glares, which was just what he had in mind.

Matt was the sort of man who could put up with a lot for a long time. He began parent training for difficult children with me after Jeb had thrown a huge tantrum at a Target store when his father tried to keep him from opening an expensive toy he had not purchased. Jeb started flailing his arms, screaming at the top of his lungs, "Let me go! Help! This man is trying to kidnap me. He's not my father. Somebody help!" After it was established at the police station that Matt was indeed Jeb's father and was not abusive, Matt decided enough was enough and set an appointment to meet me. However, before we could begin the training course, Matt took matters into his own hands. Matt had taken Jeb shopping for a new pair of shoes. Jeb wanted the most expensive sneakers made, even though he knew his father couldn't afford them. But knowing there were limitations only egged Jeb on. Matt erroneously thought if he "just explained it," Jeb would understand and be reasonable. Of course his words of reason were immediately dismissed by Jeb, who decided his father was just stingy and therefore deserving of public humiliation. Jeb started out with the usual yelling and name-calling, though this time Matt ignored him. Now Jeb was really mad, so he threw himself on the floor kicking and thrashing, and held his breath until he nearly turned blue. To Jeb's utter amazement Matt got on the floor and did the same. Wisely, the sales staff stayed out of it. At once Jeb jumped to his feet, completely shocked and horrified at his father's behavior, "Dad! Stop it! You're embarrassing me. Get up, Dad! Let's get out of here." Matt ordered the shoes he could afford for Jeb online and that was the end of store tantrums. Though Matt's approach isn't one most parents would be willing to try, I had to admit that in this case it seemed to work to at least shake up the status quo, and Jeb saw that his father was perhaps not as easily manipulated as he had come to expect. I think in this way it made our work together a bit easier. Jeb was used to being the one who embarrassed others, and really disliked it when the tables were turned, which made him more willing to stop his bratty behaviors. His dad was also willing to address some of Jeb's unresolved feelings about the divorce, which helped Jeb release some of his pent-up anger. Thereafter, the behavioral rules, expectations, and privilege-management parts of the *Dr. J Way* program fell into place with little resistance, and both Jeb and Matt felt better as their relationship improved and they could once again enjoy each other's company.

The Sulking Child: *"Poor, Pitiful Me. I Can't. You Do It."*

Perhaps one of the most challenging types of difficult child is the sulker. These children present themselves as helpless and hopeless, and then others treat them that way. It is a very effective way of getting others to do what you don't want to do: "I can't. I don't know how. You do it." Sympathy and aid are interpreted as love by these children. They revel in their dependence and freedom from responsibility. If push comes to shove they can always slump dejectedly and pull out the old standbys: "I didn't mean to," or "I can't help it." These children get their parents to do their homework, make their beds for them, fix the things they break, and take out the garbage when they "forget." Their parents learn to expect little from them, though these children expect everything from their parents. Oftentimes these children are loners who sit back and watch as other kids participate fully in activities, which makes parents feel bad for them. Parents worry that their child will be disliked, lonely, or taken advantage of by other kids, and they come to the rescue all the time, even when there is no emergency. They overprotect them to the point that they create anxiety and fears in the child, which only exacerbates the problem. These children are anything but resilient, and parents increase their dependence by their rescuing behavior.

Eleven-year-old Nick was about as smart and capable as the other boys his age, but at home you'd never guess it. At the end of the fifth grade each student was assigned a project that required selecting a figure from America history, researching that person at the library or online, and then writing a fictional letter that person might have written to a friend, describing in detail what was going on in the country at that time and what part the writer played in those events. Most of the kids were pretty excited about the project, and Nick seemed to be, too, at first. But then he dragged his feet because, as he whined to Ronda, his mom, "I just don't get it. I don't even know where to start." Per usual, Ronda zoomed in like an ambulance, with all kinds of suggestions: "Well, Nick, you have always liked Benjamin Franklin; how about writing about him?" Predictably Nick pooh-poohed her suggestions one after another and just sloughed off to his room to play video games. Ronda waited a while and then promised to take him to eat at his favorite fast-food restaurant if he would go to the library with her. Of course she would help him at the library until he had chosen a subject and found all the right materials for his project. The reference librarian recognized them right away and watched once again as Ronda gathered books, found historical information online, and printed it while Nick sat next to her looking totally uninterested. When they got home, behaving as if this were the first time this had ever happened, Ronda said enthusiastically, "There. Now you are all set to go ahead and finish your project. Just let me know if you get stuck." Nick wasn't at his desk down the hall for ten minutes before Rhonda heard his whining, "Mommm! Come here! I just can't do this by myself. It's too hard." As was her habit, Ronda dropped what she had been doing and rushed to the rescue. Nick was indeed at his desk with the books and papers, but it was obvious he had done nothing but stare at them. "Let's just get you started together," Ronda said, trying to buoy Nick up. Two hours later the letter was written, though Nick had merely been the scribe. Without so much as a "thank you," Nick complained that he was tired now and needed a break, which meant an hour of TV before bed. Ronda was worn out, but also congratulated herself for being such a good mother. Both Nick and Ronda were rewarded for a behavior pattern that in actuality was damaging to both of them, and neither of them knew it.

Worrisome, overly helpful parents who shield their children from every frustration and failure do not prepare them for the inevitable ups and downs of life. Though founded in loving concern, parents of the "poor me" kids forget that their primary obligation is to encourage skill mastery, self-reliance, and accountability. One mother I knew was still "helping" her son every day, even after he went off to college. Although he lived in a dormitory more than a thousand miles away, she called him on the phone every weekday morning at 7:45. When I inquired as to why she was doing this for an eighteen-year-old, she replied in all sincerity; "Well I just have to. After all, if I didn't call to make sure he was awake he would miss his morning classes! Then he'd flunk out! And then, well, who knows what would happen!" She gaped at me as if I had no sense whatsoever for asking such a foolish question. There was little doubt in my mind that she had been babysitting her son's responsibilities for years, and in reality, even though he was eighteen, he was no better prepared to manage adult life than an eight-year-old.

None of these real-life examples or any other difficult child behavior is easy for parents or teachers or grandparents to deal with. But all of them can be much improved if those who work closely with the child understand that even though they have difficult temperaments, when the right method that works with these kids is applied, things get better.

[Part II]

*How Children
Manipulate Situations and
Dodge Responsibility*

[3]

The Coercion Trap:
How Parents Get Lured into Arguing, Justifying, Negotiating, Nagging, Bribing, Threatening, Exploding, and Giving In

With the unintentional help of their parents, difficult-to-manage children become masters of coercion. Social learning psychologists have known since the early 1970s that beyond temperamental factors, children act as they do because of what they have observed or learned from others. All of us are learning as we go through our interactions with people, and many of those interaction patterns alter what we say and do. The good news is that children who have been inadvertently taught to argue and misbehave can be taught something better. For the most part, children who misbehave repeat the unwanted behavior because someone is reinforcing or rewarding it in some way, and they discontinue bad behavior when it is either ignored or the payoff doesn't get them what they want. Ineffective parenting behaviors often lead to noncompliance and impulsive, angry responses from difficult children, and many learn to be masters of manipulation and coercion. Rather than parents making their children behave in certain ways, it is the other way round. Once these children learn the way to become King of the Mountain they will be running the show, not you. Both parent and child draw out bad behavior in each other, and conflicts quickly escalate out of control.

> **COERCION** (*noun*): The use of express or implied threats of violence or reprisal or other intimidating behavior that puts a person in immediate fear of the consequences in order to compel that person to act against his or her will; UNDUE INFLUENCE: To force someone to act or think in a certain way by use of pressure, threats, or intimidation.*

Easily angered children read "threat" and "injustice" into all kinds of situations. They make a big deal out of little requests and needs to shift attention that others seem to be able to ignore. These children come to believe that the world is against them, which only fuels their anger. Who is the most likely "enemy"? Parents.

Though it may seem that each upset or conflict with manipulative children is different, they are very much alike and can be diagrammed. Seeing the back-and-forth process of

---

*The American Heritage Dictionary of the English Language, Fourth Edition (Boston: Houghton Mifflin, 2000).

parent-child conflict in print is very useful, because when we are captured by the tornado itself we cannot be objective enough to see what is really going on. Without a predetermined plan of response we can expect to do no better when our children defy us than someone with a stalled car who thoughtlessly opens the hood and starts pulling wires.

To have any hope of changing bad behavior, parents must become very familiar with the patterns of coercion and escalating conflict. Though you might be able to identify your child's bad behaviors in these chain reactions, it is even more important that you recognize exactly how you respond. The nasty chain of events generally starts with a parental request or command, both of which are annoying to the child who simply continues to do whatever he or she was doing:

1. PARENT REQUESTS: "Johnny, please do _____ "
2. PARENT COMMANDS: "Johnny, stop doing _____ "
3. CHILD DISREGARDS: _____

Children who want what they want on command, don't want to be interrupted, don't like routine tasks or chores, have a short fuse for anything bothersome, and don't respond well to any of these three parental actions. The noncompliant child (who erroneously but thoroughly believes any of these three parental actions is unfair) mostly ignores his or her parent. And off we go. The battle lines are drawn and the situation often plays out as follows:

THE PARENT-CHILD COMBAT ZONE

PARENT ACTION	CHILD ACTION
"Johnny, please do." (OR) "Johnny, stop doing." (OR) "No" (in response to your child's request or demand)	Ignores

PARENT RESPONSE	CHILD RESPONSE
"Did you hear me! I said, ...!!" "If you don't ...... right now, ...!!" (parent threatens)	Whine, nags, cries, argues, pesters Throws a tantrum, uses venomous talk, becomes aggressive, and/or destroys property

PARENT RESPONSE	CHILD RESPONSE
Parent manhandles the child and conflict escalates into reciprocal aggression and sometimes abuse, (OR) Parent feels threatened and worn out —**gives up, or gives in the aggression**	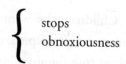 stops obnoxiousness

PARENT PAYOFF	CHILD PAYOFF
Parent relieved to be done even though child prevailed, or feels justified in having forced the child into submission	Child glad to have won, or glad the aggression/abuse is over

Notice how the chain of events ends. (This is critical.) Both parent and child are rewarded with a temporary payoff—parent is relieved that the tornado has calmed down as a result of their giving up; child wins the battle by ambushing the parent with arguments and fights instead of complying with the original instruction, or gets what he/she has been nagging for, which teaches the child how to get his or her way the next time. And, to be sure, whenever there is verbal or physical harm and abuse, everyone loses every time. Make no mistake, however, this interaction pattern is learned behavior on both parts, but parents are the adults who hold the primary responsibility to make it better. This is how the child uses coercion to get what he/she wants and to avoid having to do what he/she doesn't want to do. Each time it works the process is reinforced. The more it is reinforced the more parents feel powerless and discouraged. Fortunately what was learned one way can be unlearned and relearned another way. Seeing what actually goes on in these push-and-shove matches is the first step to handling them differently to achieve a different result.

More Coercion:
Guilt Induction Tactics

Another coercion tactic commonly used by these children is GUILT INDUCTION: *To bring about or stimulate the occurrence of guilt feelings, remorseful awareness of having done something wrong, or feeling responsible for the commission of an* *offense.** We saw a little of this manipulative strategy in the first chapter with the Sulking Child. This tactic works particularly well on parents who are predisposed to be what I call the "rescue wagon" types. These people are often anxious or natural worriers, overly responsible, carriers of other people's emotions as if they were their own, and feel duty-bound to see that everyone around them is happy all the time, usually at their own expense. Such parents are easy targets for guilt-tripping. These children's primary weapons of coercion are pouting, looking pitiful and dejected, whimpering about as though physically wounded, feeling sorry for themselves, acting the victim, hanging out their lower lips in a weepy and maudlin display, or sitting alone in a darkened room for hours on end.

These behaviors spark an immediate guilty conscience in the parent, which was exactly the intended response. The unsuspecting parents see their "poor darling" gloomy and put out, which bothers them to no end. Concluding that their child does indeed need to be rescued, they zoom in like an ambulance to cajole, sweet-talk, and do whatever it takes to make everything all better. The intent is undoubtedly based in caring, but the result is a child who never learns to deal with disappointment or to handle uncomfortable feelings. In the long run these children grow up to be needy all the time, and when they are in any need they expect someone else to take care of the problem. So, although these highly responsive parents want nothing more than a happy child, they are doing them a great disservice and raising

---

*The American Heritage Dictionary of the English Language, Fourth Edition (Boston: Houghton Mifflin, 2000).

their children to navigate their futures feeling deprived, fragile, and unable to solve their own problems.

To assess how your child may be pushing your guilty button, ask yourself the following questions:

1. What does your child **DO** (behaviors, gestures, and so on) that induces guilt in you (e.g., suddenly becomes silent and looks crestfallen)?

_____

_____

2. What does your child **SAY** that induces guilt in you (e.g., "Nobody likes me; I'll never have any friends because I don't have a new bike like everybody else.")?

_____

_____

3. What do **YOU** do or say when your child engages in these guilt-induction behaviors (e.g., "There, there; it will be okay. Maybe we can get you that new bike after all.")?

_____

_____

Take some time to link the behaviors from 1 and 2 with your responses listed above. Go back through the Combat Zone diagram on page 54 that illustrates the coercion trap and see if what you have been doing fits the pattern. Then give some thought to what you could do, say, or *not* do/say differently that might break the chain of manipulation and arguing.

For example, over ten years of living with her parents Suzette had learned that even when they were having a conversation with someone, she could interrupt and ask for something or demand their attention for any unimportant reason. I see this kind of behavior in my office all the time—parents are speaking with me about their child's behavior problems and the child calls out to the parent again and again as if they were a mile away. Ultimately one parent sighs and curtly asks, "Suzette, what is it? Can't you see I am speaking with Dr. Jacobsen?" Of course Suzette can see that a conversation is taking place—she just doesn't want to wait politely until her parents are finished. Whenever this happens I ask the child to wait outside the door and I write out what I want the parents to do instead so there is no way the child can hear it. The child is asked to return, and, sure enough, within about five minutes it happens again. But this time Suzette's parents are prepared to completely ignore her—no eye contact, no gestures, no verbal response whatsoever. Suzette persists because her parents have been allowing her to intrude on their conversations for years. She keeps it up for quite a while, assuming they will eventually come to their senses and respond as they always have in the past. But to no avail this time. Suzette's parents are astounded when she finally quits trying to get their attention and decides to go to the children's table and quietly draws pictures until the session ends.

Things I might do differently in the face of guilt induction tactics (e.g., ignore whining):

_____

_____

Danger Zone: I Can't Stand It When My Child Is Unhappy

When I encounter parents who might be justifiably termed abusive to their children, it is a tragedy to be sure. No child ever deserves to be abused, no matter how difficult they are to handle. We know that abuse only breeds violence and promotes a cycle of abuse. Far more often I see parents who subtly maltreat their children, not because they are harsh and caustic or raise a hand to them, but because they cannot tolerate even a few minutes of unhappiness in their children. By giving their children too much and bailing them out of every sticky situation they are giving too little and setting their kids up for failure. Despite obvious talents and abilities, these children often become unmotivated slackers with terrible work habits, bad attitudes, and who never seem to appreciate what they have.

These hardworking parents offer their children a comfortable—if not out-and-out lavish—existence and are beside themselves when it all goes wrong:

We have tried everything to get Tyrone to do his homework. He's so smart, but his grades are awful! He says he wants good grades and wants to go to college someday, but he doesn't do anything about it. All he wants to do is play video games and goof off with his friends. We have given him every advantage and he shows no signs of gratitude. Just the opposite. Whatever we give him or do for him, it's never enough. He doesn't do a thing to help out at home, even if we offer to pay him!

While these parents truly want to be the best they can possibly be, inadvertently they have tried to achieve being the best by means of indulgence and leniency. They can't stand it when their children aren't satisfied all the time, and in turn can't stand the guilt they feel when their children act put out.

Do you have one of these children who behaves as though he or she is royalty? You may if you . . .

- Allow your child to watch TV or play video games a great deal of the time so they won't be upset or give you any trouble.
- Regularly give in to your child's demands for new things after feigning refusal for a short time.
- Warn your child of negative consequences if he or she doesn't comply, but you rarely follow through, or the threat cannot be carried out because it was outrageous in the first place (e.g., "If you don't stop your whining you are never going to another birthday party as long as you live!").
- Indulge your child with an "allowance" that never has to be earned.
- Help your child too much with schoolwork or projects.
- Anticipate when your child is likely to drop the ball and rush in to fix it before it happens (e.g., drive all

over town late Sunday night to find the art supplies your child needs for a school project that was assigned two weeks ago and is due Monday morning).

■ Have become used to your child ignoring you when you speak and talking rudely to you.

■ Leap into action to defend your child to teachers, coaches, and others to prevent him or her from having to live with unpleasant consequences.

■ Have filled your child's room full of games, toys, electronic equipment, clothes, and other forms of entertainment.

■ Take it to heart when your child bawls you out for having unreasonable rules and not being as "fair" or "with it" as their friends' parents.

■ Work a lot of hours and feel guilty for being away, so you attempt to soothe your guilt with extravagance and leniency.

AND MOST IMPORTANTLY—

■ Can't stand it when your child is disappointed or is unhappy with you because deep down you fear that he or she will not love *you* anymore.

Let's take a closer look at this last one. It's not logical to believe that guiding a child will always go smoothly and the child will never feel frustrated or discontented. Remember, your job is to guide, to train, and, ultimately, to launch a responsible young adult into the world. If you continue to indulge your child, babify him, or take away the consequences for her irresponsible behavior, you can rest assured that in the long run you will not produce a respectful, dependable adult. You will simply have raised an older baby.

Do not make the giant mistake of connecting being loved by your child with your child showing constant satisfaction. When your adult children have grown up well they can thank you for setting limits with them and helping them to become responsible and self-reliant. For now, just know that they rely on you to guide them, and hold on to that every time they look at you as if you are the meanest, stingiest, most unreasonable person on the planet, because it is probably far from the truth. Once again, they are engaging in coercion by guilt. Do not fall for it.

Certainly give your child praise, appreciation, encouragement, hugs, and reassurance, but also love them enough to give them the ability to tolerate setbacks, deal with bad outcomes, and to own up to their choices and behaviors, both good and bad. Know for certain that when they manipulate you into indulging them and hug and love you for doing so, it is a sign of their winning far more than a sign that they love you. More times than you know the most loving thing to do in terms of their development is to hold your ground or stay out of the way if they have earned a negative consequence. In my opinion there are already enough indulged, irresponsible adult babies in the world, and we don't need any more.

What About Self-Esteem?

Parents routinely ask me about how to improve their child's sense of self-esteem. Self-esteem and how it is developed is an area that needs to be much better understood, especially when it comes to raising well-behaved children. Far too many parents think self-esteem is something that can simply be given by telling children over and over how special they are. In actuality, kids are smart enough to figure out that if the rest of their experience indicates they are disliked by their peers, doing badly in school, or can't kick a soccer ball three feet, no matter how much parents and grandparents fawn over them and talk about them as if they are angels, they aren't going to buy it. Self-esteem is the result of growing, learning, stumbling, trying again, and then mastering something that was previously difficult. We all have a self-view based in great part on how others respond to us and by how well we can do certain things. For example, an eight-year-old child who has already learned how to swim may be frightened by the very idea of jumping off a diving board. She may sit by the side of the pool for hours trying to muster enough courage to climb the ladder and try it. But when she finally heads for the ladder, climbs up, walks gingerly to the end, takes the leap, and swims to the side, her face beams with victory. Her self-esteem ("I believe in myself") just went up a notch.

By definition, *self-esteem* means: a confidence and satisfaction in oneself; self-respect; a fundamental sense of self-worth and ability. Without doubt, parents want their children to develop a healthy sense of self and confidence so that they can weather life's storms. Unlike what many parents believe, positive feedback may be given often, but self-esteem cannot simply be given.

Parents frequently ask me, "Wouldn't my child be doing better in school if he had better self-esteem?" The answer is "Yes, probably." But the stipulation is this:

> SELF-ESTEEM IS BUILT
> UPON EFFORT, MASTERY, AND
> POSITIVE FEEDBACK.

Mastery of all types of achievements, large and small, are the source of healthy self-esteem (e.g., riding a bike without training wheels, catching your first big fish, building a fort, singing in the school choir concert, learning how to properly introduce your parents to your teacher, getting all the spelling words right on the test, planting tiny seeds that in time produce real carrots, learning to play "Happy Birthday" on the piano, rocking your baby brother to sleep). The self-esteem building-block process stands to reason when you think about it. It is more likely than not that a child with a healthy sense of self-confidence will say to herself, "Yes, I think I can," when confronted with a problem that needs solving or a new skill that needs to be learned. Self-esteem heartens people to strive to improve themselves, to overcome weaknesses, and to get up and try again when the going gets tough.

Although it starts in infancy, by the age of three, children have already developed an internal and fairly substantial notion of themselves. During early child development we pay attention to what we call developmental milestones. These are markers of certain abilities that are reached by children little by little at different ages and stages (e.g., sitting up, holding a cup, pointing to things, saying "Mama" or "Dada"). Whenever a child accomplishes one of these milestones he knows it and feels pleasure in his accomplishment, which contributes to his self-esteem. Many of these developmental tasks require perseverance, which is a major ingredient in success throughout life. Take for example a child learning to walk: The child will tumble and fall, get hurt and cry, and do it all over and over again until mastery is attained. While learning to walk she is also learning about herself and her ability to improve her own skills. When others around her encourage her and allow her to continue to try despite her failures, she learns this is the natural course of progress. She also learns from the smiling faces of parents, grandparents, and caregivers that through her hard work, patience, and diligence, she is mastering something valuable for which she receives smiles, and hugs, and joyful praise. Her parents act as a mirror of her own success and her self-esteem and confidence are boosted. Healthy esteem is the result of a good balance: the child must feel loved, *and* the child must feel good about her own capacity for striving and succeeding as it is supported by family members—by parents who are not overly pushy or overly protective.

Self-esteem is not carved in stone. It fluctuates as life goes on because events and perspectives change. However, it is important to strive for the development of healthy self-esteem in children because it serves as a protective barrier against the inevitable difficulties and disappointments the world presents as they grow up. When children believe in themselves and know deep inside that they are valuable and capable they handle conflicts better and are more resilient. They also make better decisions and are less prone to negative peer pressure. And they carry with them a sense of optimism that helps them through challenging times, because by and large they believe things will turn out okay.

When children suffer from poor self-esteem they don't believe they are capable of helping themselves or solving problems with or without the help of others. They respond with intense anxiety and/or faulty judgment to seemingly ordinary stumbling blocks. They aren't sure of what to do in problem situations and don't think through possibilities or ask for help when they should. Instead they do something in a knee-jerk fashion, often making a bad choice that makes matters worse. Other children become immobilized when they are faced with problems. It stands to reason that if they think they aren't very smart or capable of working things out they might choose to withdraw or do nothing to overcome difficulties and just give up. Many of these children are liable to become depressed because feeling powerless is a key ingredient in the development of this mood disorder.

INDICATORS OF UNHEALTHY
SELF-ESTEEM IN CHILDREN

- Resists trying new things
- Negative self-comments (other than for the purpose of guilt induction to manipulate parents) such as, "I'm stupid," "I can't do anything right," or "Who cares? I don't matter anyway"
- Low frustration tolerance; gives up easily, even when a project is very important to him or her
- Seems pessimistic and fatalistic ("Things *never* work out for me")

INDICATORS OF HEALTHY
SELF-ESTEEM IN CHILDREN

- Is willing to take reasonable risks and likes trying new things
- Regularly enjoys being with others and expects to fit in
- Can enjoy playing or working on projects alone
- Tolerates frustration in a reasonable way and works through problems
- Gets upset when things go wrong without engaging in self-loathing
- Displays a generally positive outlook

HOW PARENTS CAN HELP
BUILD HEALTHY SELF-ESTEEM

- Offer praise and recognition for effort as well as success.

- Model acceptance of setbacks and mistakes; show that you can laugh off some of your own foibles; let your child see that you believe things have a way of working out even when times are rough.

- Be honest and encouraging at the same time. For instance, if your child is failing her math class let her know that you understand this subject is difficult right now and that she will need to work harder, and that you will help find a tutor or other resources so she can succeed.

- Show your child affection regularly, not just at times when he or she does something that meets with your approval. Your child needs to know deep down that he or she is loved and cared about all the time, no matter what. And say it from your heart—kids can tell the difference. Love given freely and often is perhaps the most important factor in building self-esteem.

- Validate how your child feels. For example, when a child comes home from school upset and wailing, "I hate school, and I hate my teacher, and I'm never going back there!", rather than invalidate his experience by saying, "No you don't; of course you're going back," respond only to the feelings and not to the content: "Wow. It sounds like you're really up-set." Your child needs to feel heard in order to feel understood. Naturally you are not agreeing that he will quit school and now is not the time to address his use of the word "hate." If you do that you are missing the boat entirely. Your child just needs to get credit for having the *feelings* he is feeling, and can therefore give himself permission to feel whatever he does as legitimate instead of learning to mistrust his feelings because somehow, as strong as they are, they are wrong. The resolution often takes care of itself once a child feels heard and understood. For children who are ready to start solving some of their own problems (probably much sooner than many parents think), I like to listen and then listen some more, to give a hug when the child is calm, and then say, "I see that this is hard for you, but I know you, and I trust that you can find some good way to work this out. Let me know if you would like my help and we can put our ideas together."

■ Pay attention to the ambience in your home. No one likes to dine in a restaurant that is filled with people who are disagreeable or a couple arguing at the next table, and no one wants to live in that kind of atmosphere either. Take care to assure that your child's home will be a haven—not la-la-land perfect, because conflict in families is normal, but for the most part life at home is loving, respectful, and nurturing, and completely devoid of verbal and physical abuse.

- Provide your child with opportunities to grow at his or her own pace, but with a little prodding here and there. Look for practical experiences that will help your child learn new things, deal with new people, and foster cooperation.

[Part III]

WEEK 3

Good Behavior

Required Here

[4]

What You Can and Should
Expect from Your Child

Children need to know that good behavior is a set of ground rules that they are expected to follow whether they feel like it or not. Cooperation, respect, and accountability are required first and foremost because you love your child and you recognize that your primary task as a parent is to prepare a future adult who possesses the three markers of a successful grown-up: responsibility, resilience, and self-reliance.

To establish reasonable expectations it is important to consider two fundamental factors:

- **Age-appropriateness**—Is my child developmentally capable of living up to the expectation (e.g., is my child old enough to tie his own shoes, make his bed, pick up her toys, brush her hair, dress himself, keep track of his school assignments)?

- **Aim**—Do these expectations help my child to increasingly master new skills at the appropriate age and to develop a suitable level of independence?

Maintaining some expectations seems to be easy for most parents. For example, when a child is delighted in the fact that he can tie his own shoes we don't continue to insist that we do it for him. When a child can dress herself we don't continue to help her as if she were two years old. After a child learns to ride a bike we don't run after him, ready to catch him if he falls. We get into trouble with faulty expectations when we either expect too much too soon, or we expect too little.

Age-Appropriate Expectations

As children continue to grow they develop new abilities. In early childhood these gains are often very obvious, distinct, and exciting. Parents readily remember their child's first works, first steps, and first day of kindergarten. Development continues in later years, though not usually in such clear-cut and noticeable ways. Many children progress at different rates and have differing interests, so we cannot reasonably expect all children to develop new skills and abilities at precisely the same time or to the same level. To make sure you are not expecting either too much or too little from your child, it may be helpful to become reacquainted with child developmental patterns. Because this book focuses on school-aged youngsters between the ages of six and twelve, it is useful to go over some of the common milestones children generally reach within the following age groups:

A 6-TO-7-YEAR-OLD:

+ Likes to draw, paint, and make things with his hands
+ Will practice new skills for the sake of improvement
+ Can focus on an appropriate task for at least fifteen minutes
+ Enjoys a variety of interests and can keep herself busy with her interests for a reasonable amount of time
+ Can read age-appropriate books and stories
+ Knows right from left, and day from night
+ Grasps the meaning of numbers
+ Is able to tell time by a clock
+ Can verbally describe things and explain their purpose
+ Understands three-part instructions
+ Is able to share and cooperate with others
+ May be jealous of his or her siblings
+ Likes to copy grown-ups or pretend to be an adult
+ Can play alone, though friends increasingly are valued
+ Enjoys games, including board games
+ Likes to win, and will often cheat if able to do so

A 7-TO-8-YEAR-OLD:

+ Is highly active and often learns best when actively engaged
+ Can think about his or her own actions and understand causes of events (e.g., a seven-year-old usually knows why he or she was late to school)
+ Has a strong desire for affection and attention from parents
+ Releases tension through physical activity
+ Develops new fears around school, social relationships, and disaster that replace preschool fears (ghosts, witches, and creatures of the dark)
+ Begins to learn the value of work through regular chores at home and school
+ Understands the value of money
+ Enjoys the process of work more than the product and may start many projects, but finish few unless prompted
+ Works in spurts of energy and interest
+ Is self-centered
+ Is proud of his/her developing skills
+ Gives criticism but doesn't take it well
+ Often has a hard time making choices and decisions
+ Is very interested in "rules"
+ Complains of unfair treatment
+ Wants things to be "just so"
+ Can listen well and talk with others at mealtime

+ Begins to show polite behavior and consideration of others
+ Shows friendships by sharing toys, secrets, and spending time together
+ Wants to put some distance between himself and parents

AN 8-TO-9-YEAR-OLD:

+ Can select own clothes, dress self properly, and fix own hair
+ Is able to use basic tools (e.g., screwdriver, pliers, hammer)
+ Can focus attention for about an hour
+ Enjoys collecting things (e.g., rocks, stamps, model horses, dolls, trading cards)
+ Enjoys individuals and group games and likes to compete
+ Is increasingly concerned about peer acceptance
+ Becomes more aware of own body and is often modest
+ Is often happy to be a member of a formal group (Scouts, teams, music group, chess club)
+ Attitude toward opposite sex a combination of liking and hostility
+ Enjoys dramatic play
+ Is often demanding of parents
+ Shows curiosity about nature, people, and how things work

+ Is becoming concerned about the reasons behind things
+ Tries on new behaviors "for size" (including things like swearing and defying rules)
+ Is often more polite around others than at home
+ Insists on privacy ("*My* room—keep out!")
+ Realizes parents are human and make mistakes, and doesn't like it
+ May become highly self-critical
+ May begin to sulk vs. throwing a tantrum or fighting
+ Can learn to empathize with others
+ May lack self-confidence and need support and encouragement

A 10-TO-12-YEAR-OLD:

+ Wants to be part of a group but seeks independence at the same time
+ May enjoy more complex art, crafts, building projects, or sewing
+ Can write multipart stories
+ Can follow a five-part instruction
+ Reads many kinds of materials well with understanding
+ Knows how to do basic library or online research
+ Enjoys talking on the telephone
+ Is capable of making more complex plans and carrying them out
+ Values friends and often has a "best" friend

- Can take care of pets
- Can hold and enjoy conversations with peers and adults
- Is more interested in opposite gender relationships
- Is able to focus a lot of time and energy to accomplish tasks
- Understands what a promise and the concept of trust mean
- Generally has a positive approach to life
- Finds TV and the Internet very important and identifies with characters
- Is capable of being more truthful and dependable
- Shows more self-assertion.
- May be excitable, restless, wiggly, and talk a lot
- Exhibits "off-color" humor and silliness
- May seem moody and easily frustrated
- Is very competitive, wants to excel, and may put down "outsider" kids
- May enjoy teasing and tussling with parents
- Develops a growing sense of intuition and insights about self and others
- Becomes both increasingly self-reliant and self-centered

Guiding Your Child's Development

School-age children's development is complex and their behavioral and attitudinal shifts can be quite confusing for parents. Consider these tips for fostering your school-age child's development:

- Help your child choose activities that are appropriate for his or her current abilities and then raise the bar as skills increase; don't expect too much or too little when starting new activities; try to accurately assess how your child might perform and gauge how fast and how far you can expect him or her to progress in a given amount of time.

- Encourage your child to talk openly with you about feelings; it may help to play a game with a short list of feeling words (e.g., sad, grumpy, frustrated, excited, mellow) to help your child correctly label emotions so they can be expressed appropriately. Offer suggestions for dealing with anger in healthy ways (e.g., draw a mad picture, pound on a mattress, jump rope and pound the anger into the ground).

- Encourage your child to read to you, to read alone, and offer to read to your child.

- Encourage your child to get involved with hobbies and other activities that can be done with others or on his or her own.

- Encourage physical activity as fun and a normal part of the daily routine; model this behavior yourself, so your child will learn that the joy of movement is for everyone.

- Encourage self-discipline; expect your child to follow rules that are set; reward your child when you catch him or her practicing patience, self-control, generosity, and flexibility.

- Teach your child three ways to be respectful and assertive: (a) giving thanks or praise to others ("Thank you very much for helping me with my math"; "I really like the way you did that") and accepting praise as well ("Thank you for saying that"), (b) making requests ("May I please borrow a pencil"), and (c) setting limits or saying "no" when appropriate ("I don't like playing when you keep getting so mad about losing the game, so I am going home now").

- Teach your child to listen to authority figures and to discuss with you any complaints they may have about teachers or other adults in their lives.

- Talk with your child about peer pressure and help set guidelines together that will help your child make good decisions when peer pressure occurs.

Bearing these things in mind, when it comes to what you should expect of your child my general rule of thumb is this: When children are old enough and have no impairment that would prevent them from mastering tasks and doing them on their own, for the most part parents ought to turn over that responsibility to them. If a child can get his own cereal, juice, and toast in the morning and clean up after himself, then he should be doing it. When it is reasonable for a child to learn to use the washer and dryer, that is when she starts to do her own laundry. If the child doesn't want to or forgets, so be it. The consequences will speak for themselves. Likewise, if a child knows how much time it takes to get ready for school and has an alarm that works, leave the rest to him. If he fails to get to school on time more than once or twice it will probably lead to detention, as it should. Parents are not living alarm clocks and reminder services.

With that in mind, let's create a list of tasks that are related to your child—things at home, school, sports teams, religious training, music lessons, hygiene, in the neighborhood, with pets, friends, siblings, and so on. For the moment we are only interested in making the task list. Then we can consider who should be responsible for what.

- (E.g., walk the dog after school.)
- (E.g., put out the trash can on the curb Tuesday morning on the way to the school bus.)

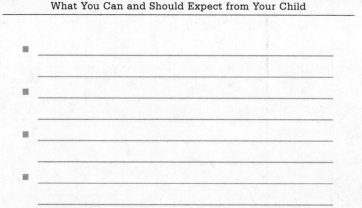

Now go back over this to-do list and check each one that you believe your child is *capable* of doing with little or no help from you. Of the ones you have checked, is your child actually expected to do them? If yes, good for you, and good for your child in the long run. If not, why? Who is taking over these responsibilities and for what reason? Is there truly a good reason? Or is it because the child balks, argues, makes a fuss, does it poorly on purpose, or just simply won't do it? If some of the items you have checked are not on your list of expectations and fall into this last category, they belong in your list of target behaviors.

Make another list of expected behaviors that are not about tasks (e.g., respectful talk, complying with requests, helping others, sharing, etc.).

- (e.g., I will come to dinner right away when called.)
- (e.g., I will talk in a normal tone and use respectful language.)
- _____
- _____
  _____

Again, check the ones you believe your child is *capable* of doing, imagining that he or she felt inclined to do so. Consider carefully the ones that are checked but not currently happening in your family. These indicate misguided leniencies that also need to go onto the target behavior list. Next you will select the top behaviors from each of the two lists as your targets for changing your child's behavior. Because you can't work on everything at once, think about which two or three from each list are the most important right now and put them in priority order.

[5]

Set Your Expectations and
Select Your Target Behaviors

From the two lists you made in the previous chapter write below the behaviors you plan to target.

Expectation # 1: _____

_____

Expectation # 2: _____

_____

Expectation # 3: _____

_____

Expectation # 4: _____

_____

Establish Specific Expectations and Clear-cut Rules

There is only one line per expectation because the aim is to create brief, clearly understandable expectations. These targets will serve as the "general" goal, and we will define them much more specifically as we proceed. To get you going, here are some examples of general expectations:

_____ (child's name) will use respectful talk.

_____ (child's name) will be considerate of others and of property.

_____ (child's name) will complete his/her homework on time as assigned.

_____ (child's name) will obey curfew rules.

_____ (child's name) will complete his/her assigned chores correctly and on time.

_____ (child's name) will use an alarm to get up on school days and will be ready in time to catch the school bus.

_____ (child's name) will put his/her belongings in the proper place at the end of each day or when asked.

_____ (child's name) will practice the piano each day as instructed.

Once these general expectations are identified we must place them within the larger context of the family, school, or community. It must be clear to your child that we all have to live up to certain obligations, take responsibility for our actions, and perform tasks we do not always like to do. Clarifying expectations will also require the other members of the family to take a look at what is expected overall, and for parents in particular to recognize what they are modeling. Research is very strong on the importance of modeling. The most powerful way that children learn is by what they see their parents doing, what they hear from their parents, and what they notice their parents do not do. It is easy to see that two parents who watch TV all weekend will be wasting their breath if they insist their child find active or productive things to do. Children learn more by example than anything else. If we want our children to talk respectfully, then we must do the same. If we want them to be hardworking and responsible, then we must exhibit those behaviors, too. If we want them to be cheerful, then we'd do well to be cheerful ourselves.

Yet even the best parent modeling is often not enough to garner good behavior in children with difficult temperaments. Nonetheless, a camera check of what you look like and sound like as parents (imagine what you would see and hear if someone invisible followed you around for a few days with a video camera) may help clean up some of the things you are unintentionally demonstrating as acceptable behavior. If parents are to have a credible set of family policies the basic ones must apply to everybody.

Policies for the Whole Family

A basic set of family policies can be very simple and to the point. Look over these examples and then create some of your own, remembering that they constitute house rules that each family member is expected to follow.

SAMPLE FAMILY RULES

1. Family members will speak to each other in a quiet tone, use language that is not offensive or threatening, not interrupt others, and will take some time apart when tempers get hot.

2. Family members will respect the property of others in the family and cause no intentional harm.

3. Family members will help out with household tasks as assigned and will do so without complaining or needing to be reminded.

4. Each family member over the age of eight will be responsible for his or her laundry.

5. Each family member over the age of ten will plan and prepare one family meal per week. The other family members will clean up on that evening.

6. (Optional for families with expectations regarding religion) Family members will participate in the following religious acvtivities:

_____ .

7. Parents make the final decision on any family rule or expectation.

This is only a sample list. Yours can be much simpler if you wish. Yet in every case it should be apparent that these expectations are not limited to one person, but in fact apply for the most part to everyone. Write your basic family policies here:

OUR FAMILY RULES

_____
_____
_____
_____
_____
_____
_____

Spell Out Behavioral Dos and Don'ts

Once each person in the family can see that certain behaviors are expected of everyone, specific dos and don'ts can be put together for each child. The best dos and don'ts are ones that can be measured (i.e., counted) and observed (as if someone were taking a video of your child's efforts). The language you use in the behavior plan should be personalized this time, not generalized to everyone, so your child knows it is expressly about him or her. Although there will need to be some words about what is *not* allowed, it is best to begin with a positive statement. This is important because otherwise your child only hears about what to stop doing, and little about what to do instead. Remember that for now all we are doing is setting up straightforward rules that your child can fully understand. We will cover what happens when rules are broken in Week 4.

Let's say, for instance, that eleven-year-old Reggie is not controlling his language or tone and has been increasingly using foul language when he gets mad. You may already have a basic family policy in place that prohibits bad or offensive language. Here is how the specific dos and don'ts might look on Reggie's behavior plan:

- I will speak in a quiet tone, use language that is not offensive or threatening, not interrupt others, and will take myself to my room to cool down when I get angry. I will not use swear words, insults, name-calling, belittling remarks, tease others, or embarrass others. In the event there is disagreement about what is acceptable language or talk, my parents will make the final decision.

Or, for example, you may want to focus on your eight-year-old daughter's habit of leaving her things lying around the house and not putting back things she takes out of cupboards, closets, and so on. You might establish something like this:

- I will hang up my coat in the closet whenever I come into the house. I will keep my bedroom floor clean and put clothes, toys, books, and other belongings in drawers, on shelves, in my laundry basket, or in the closet when not using them. I will rinse off any dishes I use and put them in the dishwasher without being reminded. I will return snack items to the refrigerator or pantry when done with them. I will promptly return things I have borrowed from others with their permission.

You will need to write out a list of specific behavioral expectations that fit with your family policies, starting with expectations that your child already fulfills. Even the smallest ones count. Add on the two or three target behaviors that you want improved and be very precise about what you expect. It may help to think in terms of: "as evidenced by . . ." If I want my child to comply better with my requests, I might write:

- I will answer my parent(s) nicely and promptly when they ask me to do something, come inside, help out, come for dinner, get ready for bed, turn off the TV, practice my violin, and in response to other requests. They will know I am responding to what they say respectfully and promptly (think, "as evidenced by" here) when they do not need to ask me more than twice, when I answer them in a quiet tone and do not complain or argue, when I go right away to where they are if I did not hear them very well instead of waiting for them to repeat their requests or come to me.

Always include in your behavioral plan those expectations that your child already fulfills successfully. That way it won't seem as though you overlook what your child does well or has already mastered. So, if your child regularly complies with requests and commands as expected, you would still include a specific expectations like the previous one. When the time comes to announce the new behavior plan you will point out to your child that some of these things are already being done very well and that you are pleased with how he or she manages these. Your child will see that there are a few important behaviors that need improvement, but in light of other successes it won't seem so impossible or such a steep mountain to climb.

Now make up a detailed set of behavioral rules for your child, beginning with ones your child complies with already. Here are some categories to consider: language, responding to requests and commands, curfew, phone use, TV or video game use, school behavior, completion of tasks, use of electronic equipment, limitations on where your child can go and with whom, help with pets, attendance of religious events, completing music or other lessons, bedtime.

_____ (your child's name) is expected to follow these rules:

_____

_____

_____

_____

_____

_____

_____

_____

_____

_____

_____

_____

_____

Review each rule to be sure it is reasonable, age-appropriate, and could be easily understood by your child in his or her language. If they are written correctly, the rules should be short, to the point, and descriptive enough so your child can readily imagine what the expected behavior looks like, sounds like, and acts like when done right. Next you will learn how these expectations will be tied to privileges, which will become one of your most influential parenting strategies.

[Part IV]

WEEK 4

The Dr. J Way:

Privileges "On"/Privileges "Off"

[6]

Privileges vs.
Inalienable Rights

It is natural for parents to want the best for their child. In fact, most of us want our children to grow up in better circumstances than we did. There is nothing wrong with that line of thinking. Nonetheless, this charitable approach to child rearing can easily become exaggerated, in which case you will experience dreadful pangs of guilt every time your child pouts or looks disgruntled. Bear in mind, as we saw in Chapter 3, guilt induction is a primary coercion tactic children use to get what they want.

One of the cornerstones of effective parenting is a clear-cut understanding of what constitutes a privilege. This may seem like a no-brainer, but I assure you it is not so simple. Whether low income or wealthy, the vast majority of parents I have worked with over the years indulge their children in ways they don't recognize. Worse yet, they fail to realize the tremendous influence privilege control has on behavior. In nearly every case I've seen children who have many more privileges than parents identify. Separating privileges from rights is essential because allowing and disallowing privileges is a fundamental part of the *Dr. J Way* to better behavior. Any child who can convince you that a privilege is an inalienable right has the upper hand. If you believe you cannot or must not take away privileges you will fail to use the most effective tool for shaping your child's behavior.

Your Child's Rights

Because control over your child's privileges is key to better behavior, it is important to clarify the difference between a *right* and a *privilege*. Your child has a right to expect you to be a responsible parent. It is your legal duty to provide:

1. Adequate shelter (which does *not* mean a professionally decorated room full of toys, TV, computer, stereo, phone, video games, and so on).

2. Adequate clothing (which does *not* mean $150 athletic shoes or designer jeans).

3. Adequate food (which does *not* mean you have to spring for pizza delivery, McDonald's, or five liters of soda per week).

4. Access to education (which does *not* mean you must drive your child to school when he or she misses the

bus or for you to deliver homework or lunches that were forgotten).

5. Access to basic health services (whether or not your child resists it).

6. *No* abuse (there is no "*maybe*" about this one).

Privileges Defined

As a parent, the six obligations listed above are your fundamental duties, which are indeed your child's rights. ***Everything else is a privilege.*** Certainly I don't believe that the bare-bones parental responsibilities most state laws set forth represent the sum total of good parenting. But it is essential that you know where the line is between your responsibilities and all the benefits you provide for your child. Think about that for a minute. Take a look around at what your child has and consider all the things you do for your child that go beyond the list of basic duties. Quite a lot, isn't it? Television time, video games, computers, stereos, phones, toys, books, games, scooters, climbing gyms, bikes, Rollerblades, soccer equipment, outings for basketball games, art supplies, lunches made, laundry done, favorite snacks, rides to places your child wants to go, trips to the amusement park, having friends in for a sleepover, stories at bedtime, autographed jerseys, coaching the Little League team, baking cookies, marketing, helping with the class party, assisting the teacher on a field trip, cleaning and then cleaning some more, working hard to pay the bills, planning and going on vacations, and on and on and on. . . .

Isn't It Mean to Take Away My Child's Privileges?

What is the worst thing that could happen if your child temporarily lost privileges? Yes, your child will undoubtedly gawk at you as if you had suddenly lost your mind or become possessed. To recoin a familiar saying, hell hath no fury like an entitled child who feels deprived! The over-the-top outrage such children can stage is truly something to behold. I have worked with families whose "willful" or "spirited" child can tantrum for up to an hour or more—ranting, screaming at an ear-piercing decibel level, kicking, biting, and throwing things around including themselves. One memorable child was able to put on such a show of furious indignation that he writhed about on the floor turning blue in the face to the point where his parents were afraid if they didn't give in he would injure himself. Of course, whenever a parent or caregiver believes a child is so out of control that he or she is likely to cause harm to himself or someone else, adults need to step in and take charge.

I also recall a twelve-year-old girl who was so irate when her parents reasonably refused to let her attend a rock concert without an adult along that she locked herself in the bathroom shrieking that she had a razor blade and was going to slash her wrists unless they let her go. Despite her best efforts, instead of giving in to her demands her savvy parents took her to the hospital where she spent the weekend in a locked psychiatric unit on a seventy-two-hour hold. I can assure you the incident was not repeated.

Regardless of your child's dramatic, if not downright hysterical, response to privilege removal, I know of no child who has died from doing without the extras for a while. The important thing here is to remember your role as parent—to launch a responsible, self-disciplined, capable person into adulthood. This doesn't mean you can wait until your child is fifteen or sixteen to take this seriously. Believe me, you do not want to allow today's degree of arguing, defiance, tantrumming, and obnoxiousness to go unchecked into adolescence. Just imagine a surly teenager with a long history of getting his way who is now big and strong. In response to your "no," he is smashing things around, calling you all kinds of foul names, telling you what a horrid parent you are, shaking his fist in your face, punching a hole in the wall, threatening to run away, or threatening you. You will have a big problem on your hands. What will you do when you can no longer take your child to his room, or pick her up and carry her kicking and screaming out of the store?

When a young child is regularly behaving badly, throwing tantrums, or losing control, it is never a good idea to wait to see if it is just a passing phase. The earlier parents step in to alter bad behavior the better. It is best to start out with reasonable and fairly inflexible rules and expectations and loosen up gradually over time *only* as your child matures, demonstrates proper behavior and good self-control most of the time, and earns your trust. As a parent, you must be in control of your child's privileges. Think of privileges flowing from you like water. You must have your hand on the faucet that turns access to privileges on and off because this is the pressure valve that turns bad behavior into good. How? First, by allocating your child's privileges on a contingency basis—good behavior, and privileges are on; bad behavior, and privileges are off. Over the years I have heard so many parents lament, "We have tried everything, and nothing works!" The *Dr. J Way*, either "all on" or "all off" works and works well, even with the most defiant, obstinate child.

Know Your Child's Privileges

Now we are ready to put what you have learned to paper. Remember, privileges are *everything* that is not included in the list of basic child rights. Even though your child may define things like soda pop, use of the computer, or rides to a friend's house as ordinary events, they are privileges nonetheless. List your child's privileges in each category below. Remember, if it is not on the short list of children's basic rights on page 98, it is most likely a privilege. Try to be as thorough as possible (you may need extra paper if your child has many privileges).

Objects (e.g., toys, games, TV, computer, phone, sports equipment, clothes, money):

_____
_____
_____
_____

Treats (e.g., favorite foods, soda, snacks, dessert, story read at bedtime, fun outings):

_____
_____
_____
_____
_____

Access and Permission (e.g., going to the park, going outside to play, using dad's tools, talking on the phone, use of electricity and computer, getting rides to events, having friends over or visiting them):

_____
_____
_____
_____
_____

Your list need not be exhaustive at this point. You can always add privileges as you go forward.

[7]

How to Apply the Dr. J Way *Step-by-Step and Avoid Five Common Parenting Mistakes*

The *Dr. J Way* in a Nutshell

Once you have established behavioral expectations, you will let your child know that cooperation means that all privileges will be his or hers to enjoy *(Privileges ON)*, but if they do not hold up their end of the bargain they will not be allowed to enjoy *any* privileges *(Privileges OFF)*. When privileges are either "on" or "off," it's all or nothing, and it will have a dramatic effect on your child's behavior.

You will need to announce your new behavioral expectation plan to your child, and will learn how to present it in Chapter 8. First, it is essential that you understand the process yourself and fully understand what you will do each step of the way.

STEP # 1
Give No-Nonsense Requests and Commands

The *Dr. J Way* uses very few words, and sometimes none at all. When your child misbehaves the focus must remain on that behavior, *not* on you or the reasons for your actions. The fantastic bonus is when this plan is put into action you can say farewell to prompting, reminding, pleading, bribing, nagging, and lecturing for good!

Here is how to do it. When you are asking your child to do something or to stop doing something, be sure you have your child's attention, then very clearly and simply say:

"(Name), please **do** _____."
OR
"(Name), please **stop** _____."

If your child does not comply immediately, you repeat once, but not in exactly the same way. With firmness (not yelling), instruct your child as follows:

"(Name), **do** _____ *right now*."
OR
"(Name), **stop** _____ *right now*."

STEP # 2
Two Strikes and Your Child Is Out

Whenever privileges are removed or restored they all need to go together. Privileges are either *entirely "on"* **or** *entirely "off."*

The *Dr. J Way* has no in-betweens, no dribbling of privileges one by one. Research is clear that swift, high-impact consequences are far more effective. Besides, it makes your life so much simpler. You will no longer need to feel pressured to come up with yet another way to deal with each and every bad behavior. With no more trial-and-error you can stick with a system that works.

Step # 3
Dull and Dreary Detention: Time-out Is Not *About Time*

Forget the clock. Follow the steps described below for putting your child into a time-out. But before you do, think carefully about where you will put your child. Dull and dreary detention is a cardinal rule of the *Dr. J Way*. The time-out location must be void of anything remotely interesting. No toys, games, TV, magazines, drawing materials, playing cards, computer, phone, snacks, or gadgets. To be effective detention must be utterly boring and cut off from other people—nothing is allowed in this place except unfinished homework that can be done in that location and does not require the use of a computer. If your child's room is full of these things, perhaps a laundry room or staircase or kitchen table would work better. The essential feature of the time-out space is that it should not place your child within eyesight of others or have any materials handy that would be entertaining.

As you escort your child to detention, calmly and firmly announce, "Privileges are off. You are in time-out." *Do not* talk to your child in detention or respond to his tantrums or melodramatic complaints of injustice in any way unless you or your child or valuable property is being endangered. *No* discussion, explanations, or conversation. If your child is highly aggressive or destructive when he doesn't get his way, you will need to plan accordingly by making the detention room as hazard-proof as possible. If your child does not voluntarily stay in the designated room or detention place you may need to position a chairback or something else under the doorknob so your child cannot leave. If your child is not in a separate room (e.g., at the kitchen table or on a stair step), you may need to sit behind your child (not within eyesight) to reseat him should he get up.

If your child is small enough to physically constrain and is becoming dangerous you may do a basket hold. Sit tailor-fashion on the floor with your child seated in between your legs with his back to you. Wrap your arms and legs around your child firmly enough to restrain him without hurting him. If your child is a biter you can do the same thing only using a beach towel around his arms instead of your arms. Under no circumstances should you speak to your child. You will release him when he has calmed and then return him to detention without comment.

Step # 4
Owning the Problem: Why Your Child Needs to Explain What He/She Did Wrong

In my experience, the key to developing a proper anticipation of consequences and better judgment in children is more than just experiencing the consequences. If a child can be taught to identify his or her feelings and develop emotional awareness as the basis of emotional self-management, then surely he or she can be taught to identify good and bad behaviors and connect them to privileges being on or off. By helping children reason out these things we provide them with a framework for taking responsibility for their own choices and actions more and more often. (See task #2 on the next page.)

STEP # 5
Restoring Privileges: the Four Earn-Back *Tasks*

What happens when the messy part is over and your child has calmed down? Do you simply restore privileges and call it a day? No. Your child's best opportunity to learn from the experience would be lost that way. To have privileges restored your child must complete four *earn-back* tasks. Be certain that your child thoroughly understands what is expected and how each of the four tasks is to be done. For the child who is truly forgetful or for children prone to manipulating you with convenient "forgetting," it is best to have the four tasks written on an index card that can either be posted in the time-out place or given to your child at the time of detention. If she throws a hissy fit and tears up the card, so be it—she will just have to piece it together. If you believe your child truly can't recall or make use of the index card, upon respectful request you may offer another card under the door—but without discussion.

Your child must remain in detention until he or she has demonstrated that he or she is not agitated, enraged, or out of control. Your child may then politely ask to be released from detention. If you agree, while blocking your child from going anywhere or doing anything else, and no discussion, your child may proceed to the four tasks. For older children who clearly get it or for younger children after they have been through the drill a couple of times, do not prompt the child about what to do. The four earn-back tasks must be completed in order.

FOUR EARN-BACK TASKS

1. Your child must calmly and respectfully request to be let out of detention. If you believe your child is surly or still agitated ignore the request.

2. As soon as you agree to allow the child out of detention he or she must sincerely and appropriately apologize precisely as follows: "I am sorry for _____ (a specific statement of what was done wrong) and I know that is wrong because _____ (e.g., "it hurts people's feelings," "I am expected to do my chores correctly and on time," "it is wrong to be disrespectful," "I am not allowed to take things that don't belong to me without permission").

3. If the problem that sent your child to detention was failure to do a chore or to do it on time, then that chore must be immediately completed as expected under your supervision and without discussion. If

the misbehavior was something other than a chore, such as hitting a sibling or swearing at you, obviously your child can't undo the damage. In such cases the child is escorted to the person involved to make proper amends. Sometimes it is also a good idea to require your child to write a paragraph or give a short verbal report on the effects of the bad behavior and what should have been done differently that are good behavior options for the future. Older children may need to do some research, which you will have to supervise (e.g., write a report on the dangers of smoking cigarettes).

4. The last step is important because it reconnects good behavior with privileges. It is not good enough for your child to simply go back and do what should have been done in the first place. Because a rule was broken your child must complete an extra earn-back chore of your choosing. The chore must be age-appropriate and doable by your child. It should also be somewhat unpleasant (e.g., scrubbing the toilets, cleaning out and organizing the "junk" drawer, sweeping the garage, folding the laundry, wiping up the kitchen floor, washing out the garbage cans). You may have your child pick from a number of tasks you have written in advance on slips of paper and placed in a box or other container. Or you may give your child a choice between two chores that you have selected. Or you may simply assign a par-

ticular chore. Any arguing about the selected chore will result in a second chore. You will need to supervise the completion of the earn-back task. If done properly you do nothing more than say, "good work; your privileges are now back *on*." If your child does not follow through as expected, is insolent, or tries to argue with you during this process, silently escort him or her back to detention to start over.

For easy reference, the Four Earn-Back Tasks are listed in Appendix B on page 187.

Common Parenting Mistake #1: Talk, Talk, and Then More Talk

I can't count the number of times parents complain to me, "We just can't get through to her. We tell her over and over, but it doesn't matter one iota. We sit her down and go over all the reasons why we have this rule and how it is for her own good. But she just keeps doing it!" This is definitely a case of more being worse, not better. Though I don't always object to parents explaining to their child the reasons for parental decisions and rules, it backfires when you are in the midst of disciplining your child. Worse yet, like a naïve witness being questioned by an opposing attorney in court, when you go on and on explaining, justifying, and lecturing you are playing right into your child's hands. You are inviting your child to argue with your rules or discredit them. They will make every attempt to override your authority, delay consequences, frustrate, confuse, and exhaust you until you either give up or give in.

Common Parenting Mistake #2:
Tolerating Foot-dragging and Noncompliance

If you have given your child two chances to follow your instructions and he or she does not, there are no more chances. The privilege faucet is *off* without delay. Go and get your child and with no discussion escort her to your designated place for time-out. This should be a place where your child has access to no items of entertainment and no conversation will be allowed. Once the child is in the time-out space there is no further conversation. When you child breaks a rule, announce in a normal tone: "All privileges are *off* and you are in detention because you . . .", and leave it at that. No more words no matter what your child does, however much he or she protests— just keep on moving your child along toward your predetermined detention place. If your child must use the bathroom during detention, do not allow her to lock the bathroom door. Escort her there and back without words and then immediately disengage and ignore her.

Common Parenting Mistake #3:
The Dribble Method and Making Time-out About Time

Just like with a leaky faucet, while bad behavior may seem to be shut off, it quickly seeps out again. Taking away privileges one at a time is a stopgap measure, because the child is hardly ever seriously put out and therefore has little motivation to correct the bad behavior. For instance, if you punish your child by taking away phone privileges, what is the effect when she can simply go online or ride her bike to her friend's or play video games until the upset blows over? Consider all of your child's privileges as a package deal. When you present the *Dr. J Way* to your child as you will be instructed in Chapter 8, your child will know exactly which behaviors are expected and which are unacceptable. Children begin to take responsibility when they see the connection between *their* choices and actions and access to privileges. When parents and I announce the plan together in my office I always tell the kids, "Having access to your privileges is entirely up to *you* now. If *you* want to keep all these wonderful things that are important to *you*, all you have to do is behave according to your family's rules. It's that simple." They almost always don a grin of victory because initially they interpret this as carte-blanche freedom to do whatever they please whenever they please, and to get out of anything they don't want to do. It's not so. I make sure they understand that their parents will follow the plan to a T, and that it is *the child's* choices that will determine whether privileges will be on or off. This way when things don't go well and your child's privileges are removed it is no surprise (though at first he or she will undoubtedly act astonished). Because you will be explaining it to them in detail, they will know in advance precisely what will happen, and all you do is implement the rewards or consequences.

If your child learns that all he has to do when he misbehaves is wait out the clock, why do anything more? How does time change unwanted behaviors? Moreover, this is not how things work in the real world. If I fail to pay my electric bill for two months more time won't help me a bit. If I was such a reckless driver that a judge revoked my license, I could sit around in the courthouse all day, but that wouldn't get my license back. Remember, you are not a service center, your job is to provide your child a launching service into responsible adulthood. The whole point of this is to help the child make the connection between behavioral choices and consequences, and that bad behavior requires the earning back of privileges and in turn the rebuilding of trust.

Common Parenting Mistake #4:
Ownership of the Problem Is Not Required

Far too many parents not only use time-outs incorrectly, they fail to have their child make a mental connection between bad behavior and loss of privileges. Even as early as half an hour after the infraction that got them into time-out, most of the highly challenging children I work with would never be able to tell you *what* they did wrong, much less *why* it's wrong and *how* they should have behaved differently. If we do not teach our children to reason through what goes on in their lives, how can we expect them to anticipate the consequences of their actions on themselves and others? Will they even know that alternative behavior choices exist? How will they come to believe that they are capable of making good choices when they have an urge to behave badly? Children must be taught to articulate where they went wrong and to understand their options and how the choices they make lead to positive or negative outcomes.

Common Parenting Mistake #5:
Effortless Restoration of Privileges

When parents do all of the above and fail to require the child who misbehaved to "earn back" privileges we do them a great disservice. They will learn from the experience that putting in time is sufficient when they have done wrong. They also learn that privileges naturally return again as if they were a God-given right and that there is no need to do anything to restore them.

Remember, earning privileges is something they will encounter in the real world. If you decide you don't feel like going to work for a few days, is that okay? Do you not need to use vacation or sick time that you have *earned?* If you do yard work for a living and you fail to show up for three customers because you felt like doing something else, would you reasonably expect to be paid anyway? When someone abuses driving privileges, gets ticketed several times, and a judge revokes his license, does it just come back in the mail a few days later? *No,* of course not.

The earn-back procedures are a vital part of the *Dr. J Way* because your child needs to learn—after the fact at first—how to anticipate the consequences of his or her actions and inactions. Rather than being a nonthinking child who continues to immaturely believe that he or she gets into trouble simply because they were caught, or because some adult was unfair, your child will develop a sense of ownership over both good behavior and bad. Most importantly, while removal of privileges is directly linked with unacceptable behavior as it should be, likewise making amends and doing things correctly is directly linked with restoration of privileges. These connections are vital for the development of a proper conscience, accountability, and self-control.

Seven-year-old Tricia's mom was having trouble getting her to stop doing what she wanted and shift directions when it was time to do something else. Her mom calmly asks her to put away her toys because it is time for a bath. Tricia doesn't want to stop playing, stomps her feet, and hollers, "No!" In a firm yet neutral tone Mom commands her to pick up her toys right now. Tricia now picks up a doll and flings it with all her might in the direction of her mother. Tricia is escorted to her dull and dreary time-out place and all privileges are off. She already knows the rules to earn her way out. After about ten minutes Tricia's mother can hear that she has calmed herself down. Through the door Tricia politely asks if she can come out. Mom opens the door and Tricia, who is relatively new at this, gets some prompting from her mom about what she must say. In response, Tricia says, "I'm sorry, Mom. I know that what I did, yelling and throwing things, are bad behaviors. And I know it's wrong because it's not respectful to yell at people and throwing things can hurt. A better choice would have been to say I am mad that I have to stop playing and then count each toy as I put it away, telling myself that I don't have to choose to get into trouble. That would have been better, wouldn't it, Mom?" Tricia's mom hugs her and tells her that she is very pleased with how Tricia calmed herself down and was able to tell her all this. Then the remainder of the earn-back process I outlined proceeds.

I realize that to many parents out there Tricia's reasoning seems pretty sophisticated, but you would be surprised how easy it is to get kids to do this with a little practice. They are following a formula that helps them link their behaviors to privileges being either on or off, and they are creating a habit of thinking through possibilities that are connected to consequences, so that more and more of the time they can catch themselves on the verge of a bad choice earlier in the process.

[Part V]

*Argue No More! Setting
the Plan in Motion*

[8]

Presenting the Plan
to Your Child

Many plans for changing behavior fail from the start because they are not specific enough or are too negative. Before explaining your behavior plan to your child or children, go over your ground rules one more time. Think about what exactly you want to see your child doing. Use the following checklist to review your objectives:

☐ Does your behavior plan start with a positive list of general family policies that show how all family members are expected to behave?

☐ Is each behavioral rule specific enough for your child to know exactly what is expected and what is not allowed?

Examples of rules that are *not* specific enough to be effective:

> *Suzanne will be more responsible.*
> *Leroy will help out around the house.*
> *Tina will play nicely with her younger sister.*

Examples of rules that are specific because they nail down what the child is to do and not do, and are therefore more likely to succeed:

> *Suzanne will have all her school books, papers, assignments, and materials in her backpack and at the front door ready to go each night before she goes to bed.*

> *After dinner on Mondays, Wednesdays, and Fridays, Leroy will clear all the dishes from the table after dinner, scrape the plates and pans into the disposal, rinse all the dishes and pans, load them into the dishwasher and run it, and wipe off the table and counter with paper towel and kitchen counter disinfectant cleaner.*

> *When Tina plays with her younger sister, she will use friendly talk and gestures (normal tone, pleasant face, kind words, no pushing, grabbing things, or hitting), show patience when her sister is learning something new (no name-calling or bossing), and will take a time-out in her room to calm down if she becomes frustrated or angry.*

☐ Are you targeting only one or two behaviors for change? (*Attempting to get your child to change many habits at*

once is unreasonable and will surely lead to failure. Re-
member, you are targeting only one to two behaviors right
now. Other behavioral goals can be added later. Try to
make your rules as brief as possible so the task of improving
will not overwhelm your child and so tracking change will
be easy.)

☐ Have you written your rules as carefully as possible to
(a) make them positive vs. negative *(describe each de-*
sired behavior in upbeat language), and (b) ensure that
your child will be able to easily grasp and create a mental picture of what you want him or her to do and not
do? *(Would others be able to quickly understand your*
rules? You may want to go over them with a friend to be
sure.)

☐ Have you included some behavioral expectations that
your child has already mastered successfully? *(To build*
optimism in your child and to show that you care about
the good things he or she already does, you need to include
at least two or three behaviors for which your child can re-
ceive immediate appreciation. You can remind your child
that he or she can improve other behaviors and learn new
behaviors just like he or she did with these successes.)

☐ Can goal achievement be measured? *(You cannot know*
if your child's behaviors are improving unless you can
track what he or she is and is not doing. For example, if
your goal is to have your child make up his bed before go-

ing to school each morning, you will need to pay attention to his behavior and chart whether or not he completes the task in the way you have explained it and practiced beforehand. Specific ideas for charting will be presented in Chapter 10. Review each goal to be sure the desired behaviors can be counted or measured in some way. Think in terms of: How often? How long does it last? On a scale of 1 to 10, how intense or unruly is the behavior?)

☐ Have you set your goalposts? (To know that progress is happening we have to be able to measure behaviors. To measure them we must be very clear about where we are when we begin. Using the example with Suzanne above, suppose Suzanne has been forgetting some of her school materials or her entire backpack more days than not. Estimate about how many school days per month this has been happening, including the days she pulls things together at the last minute but does so in a fit of turmoil. If you concluded that this occurs about three to four mornings per school week, set your baseline goalpost at four. It is helpful to start on the higher end if you aren't sure improvement is likely to occur sooner. Then determine a reasonable and doable level of improvement. Though it would be nice, never forgetting her things is not a very reasonable expectation for a child. You may want to set the end goal as fewer than two times a month, and when you announce the plan to her, explain that if and when she does forget her things she will have to deal with the consequences at school on her own.

☐ Do you fully understand how to use the time-out method and manage the use of privileges? *(If you don't fully grasp the* Dr. J Way *steps, you cannot expect your child to understand what to do or expect, and it is likely that you will become inconsistent, which is a disaster for training new behaviors. Before you begin, go over the steps on pages 105–111 again and check to see that you are prepared by explaining them in detail to a friend.*

(Appendix C on page 189 provides a fill-in-the-blank version of a behavior plan that I have used with many families. If you choose to use it, include all the categories that apply in your case, and exclude others that don't apply. However, I recommend that if your child is already behaving well in some of the pertinent areas listed (e.g., curfew), then leave it in as a positive part of the discussion when you present your expectations. That way your child will see that you are not focusing entirely on unacceptable behavior, and that they are receiving credit for good behaviors already in place.)

When and How to Begin

Once your behavior plan meets these requirements you are nearly ready to go. The next step is to decide when to set the plan in motion. Here are some things to consider to help you get off to a good start:

■ Begin the plan as soon as possible when it appears your child is in a reasonably good mood—not in the midst of a tantrum, when either of you is worn out, when you are dealing with other children's needs, or when it will be some time before you can actually start the plan.

- Mentally rehearse your explanation, visualizing yourself as calm, straightforward, firm, and not distracted by your child's attempts to interrupt or argue.

- Sit at a table to establish a businesslike atmosphere. Tell your child that you have a new plan that will make things go a lot better. Start by reassuring your child that it is your job to help her grow up well, and that as a parent you are the one who sets the rules. Encourage your child by saying that you believe in her, and that you know she can succeed and do better a little at a time. Tell her that in order to do so you have a new plan for the family.

- Inform your child that his job is to listen carefully without interrupting as you explain the new plan.

- Go over the basics of the plan without elaborating or giving examples of past behaviors. Speak confidently and without blame.

- When you have finished your explanation, make it very clear to your child that these rules are not open to discussion. Ask if he or she understands each rule. If you are uncertain if everything is understood, ask your child a bit later to paraphrase what is expected.

(If at any time the presentation breaks down, send your child to a time-out place and wait until he or she calms down.

If your child is very disruptive and willful, you may need to explain the plan in smaller segments.)

You should explain consequences for breaking rules after the rules are laid out. If your child is doing well and taking in these new rules, take a twenty-minute or half-hour break. After the break, ask your child to come back to the table and go over the details of Privileges "On," Privileges "Off," and the Four Earn-Back Steps to get out of time-out and earn back privileges. It is best to have copies of the Four Earn-Back Steps to give to your child (see Appendix C, page 189), written in language that you know your child will be able to easily read and understand.

Present A United Front

If you have more than one child, it may be best to announce your rules on the weekend when your other children are away at a relative's house or have been taken out for the day. If you are a two-parent family, it is important that both parents are present when the plan is announced, that both parents fully understand and agree upon the specifics of the plan, and that they decide ahead of time who will do the talking. Presenting a united front is essential for children with difficult temperaments who are already masters at manipulating others to get what they want. If it appears as though the two of you disagree, or that you are not equally committed to the plan, you can be sure your child will use that to his advantage. Children with difficult temperaments are highly aware of discrepancies and will always look for ways to divide and conquer, so you must make it very clear to your child at the beginning and throughout the process that it is the two of you who are in charge and in agreement with the rules and consequences. A united front is also needed in charting progress, delivering consequences, ignoring, and doling out praise and rewards. In a two-parent family, both parents need to be prepared to step in at any moment to take over one of these tasks.

If there are other caregivers (grandparents, babysitters, and so on) who are regularly involved with your child, let them know the details of the plan and precisely how you would like them to be involved. Although you cannot be sure teachers and grandparents will necessarily agree to be on board with your plan, at least they will know what you are trying to accomplish and can look for ways to encourage improvement in those areas while your child is under their supervision. If others who care for your child are not willing to participate, it may be wise to avoid the confusion of conflicting expectations while you are getting started by trying to see alternative arrangements for the first week or so.

Warning! Expect a Flameout

It is likely that your child's tantrums will *temporarily* get worse before they go away. When you know a flameout is likely, although it may still come as a surprise, you will be in a much better position to react wisely if a response is well-thought-out in advance. Remember, your child has a history of bad behavior that has been reinforced through the unintentional reactions of others. Your child has *learned* that arguing, throwing things, guilting you, whining, and becoming aggressive all *work!* This is not a child who will be talked out of behaving that way, because it has been such a winning game plan. That is precisely why all the talking was so ineffective. Your child has used coercion tactics again and again because they got your child what he or she wanted. It stands to reason that when *you* change how *you* respond, your child will be completely baffled. Because you are not responding in ways your child expects, he or she will escalate in an effort to *make you* give in or give up as before.

Be ready. Children who were not previously physically aggressive, may become that way in an effort to get *you* back under their control. Children who have been explosive and aggressive in the past may get worse to the point that other adults need to intervene, or the police need to be called. If your child has resorted to physical violence in the past, prepare yourself well by having hurtful objects put away, having other adults who can calmly help out be there to support you, and have at the ready crisis contact numbers to call if immediate help is needed.

Luckily, most flameouts are not dangerous. Remember, it is critical that unless there is true danger, your response is to *utterly ignore* the drama. The vital reason for ignoring is: If you respond to the amplified tantrum by giving in, you have now unleashed a monster—your child will have learned that in order to get you to do what he or she wants, this new and much more spectacular form of tantrum is the way to get it. And that is the new level of obnoxiousness you will get from then on.

So, set aside the time to sit down with your child and walk him through the new plan. Be sure that you are comfortable with the steps and information so that you can confidently explain them. Be forewarned, once the plan is in place your child may escalate previously obnoxious or even violent behavior in order to return to the status quo. Hold your ground—this new plan will work out and make a positive change in your child and your household.

What to Do if You Are Very Angry and About to Lose Control

Many parents find this initial phase difficult, which is why it is so important that you remind yourself that you must stay strong and ride out any flameout storm that occurs. These are always temporary if you just don't allow yourself to give in. Unfortunately, some parents who have a tendency to be short-tempered become so exasperated with this that they run the risk of demonstrating a tantrum of their own. If you know that you have a short fuse and it is possible that your child's temporary escalation of obnoxiousness may push you into an angry outburst, you also need to be prepared ahead of time to stop it before it starts. Here are some tips to avoid a blowout of your own:

1. Put your hands in your pockets or clasp them tightly together behind your back.

2. Get away from the situation if you can—go to another room.

3. Close your eyes and count backwards from 100 by fours—doing the math in your head will require enough concentration to help your deescalate.

4. Manage your breathing—take in deep breaths slowly through the nose and let your breath out slowly with a relaxing sigh.

5. Think about what should happen now—remember, you have a plan, so use it.

[9]

Selective Attention and Reinforcement

Privilege management can serve as a powerful behavior-change tool. Likewise, the proper application of selective attention is a comparable tool that is indispensable for bringing about behavior change in children. With the Coercion Trap in Chapter 3, you saw how children cleverly engage parents when they want something, but they pay no attention when they don't want to do something they're asked to do. Children are not the only ones who can use this technique. Parents can turn the tables on selective attention and learn how to outsmart unruly children at their own game. Once you understand how attention works to shape behavior, you will be equipped to respond mindfully and not simply react in knee-jerk fashion to each and every child behavior. To overcome knee-jerk reacting that only serves to stoke the fires of bad behavior, you will need to master the art of selective attention.

How and when and why we pay attention to a child determines which behaviors will be encouraged and therefore continued. To avoid supporting and reinforcing unwanted behavior by mistake, you have to understand what the child is experiencing each time you dole out or withhold attention. Correctly responding to different child behaviors makes a huge difference in the behaviors your child will consistently engage in.

For example, when Marcus turned six years of age, he began to clown around for attention by making faces at people in grocery stores and for his parents' friends when they came for dinner. Everyone thought this was cute and funny, and Marcus enjoyed the attention and laughter he received. This was all fine and good until he started making obnoxious noises, sticking out his tongue at people, and distracting people with his antics in restaurants and at the library. Suddenly it wasn't fun or entertaining anymore and Marcus's parents told him to stop it. By now the behaviors had been so well reinforced that their words had no effect. When Marcus's parents explained this to me, I let them know that in order to extinguish these unwanted behaviors they would need to entirely ignore him when he acted up—no eye contact, no comments, and no gestures in response that would serve as reinforcing attention. If his behaviors started to escalate out of control or bother others, Marcus was to be picked up and silently removed from the situation. Sure enough, his tricks worsened for a few days, and then, as Marcus's parents held their ground, they stopped altogether. They also started praising Marcus for polite behaviors in public, which he loved, and which was the reinforcement for the behaviors they wanted from him.

The Power of Ignoring

In my opinion, one of the most influential reactions to a child's behavior is also the most underutilized by parents. The power of ignoring cannot be overstated. If your child has thrown more than one or two tantrums, has badgered you mercilessly until you gave in, or has whined in response to your every request to do something to the point that you just do it yourself, you have probably left one of your best power tools in the toolbox: ignoring. Unwanted behaviors that *can* be ignored and *should* be ignored include:

Whining	Grumbling
Pouting	Complaining
Sulking	Nasty remarks
Nagging	Crying jags
Pleading	Badgering

Don't let yourself be fooled into thinking that these behaviors are anything but attempts at coercion, especially if they occur in the face of your request or of your denial of what the child wants. Remember, to a difficult-temperament child, every time you say, "do—," or "stop—," or "no," the child interprets it as outrageously unfair. However, you are the parent, and you have every right to expect things from your child and to set limits as well.

Take a minute to look at each of the obnoxious behaviors listed above and you will see that they are all actions a child takes with the sole purpose of bothering you to the point that you give her what she wants right now. These purposeful acts of annoyance nearly always elicit from an unknowing parent just what the child wants most—attention. However, years of child behavior research has determined that *attention* fans the flames of obnoxiousness and reinforces bad behavior. A fire without fuel will eventually extinguish itself, so, if we want better behaved children, we need to ignore the pouting, tantrums, and other antics that are obnoxious. There are two steps to effectively ignoring these behaviors:

> ### STEP # 1
>
> ### IGNORE UNWANTED BEHAVIORS
>
> *Don't look. Don't discuss.*
> *Don't get involved. Don't reengage.*

Now, because this is easier said than done, especially when your child is kicking up a fuss and you are worn out from the day (which is their favorite time to manipulate you), you must be very clear about each step of the ignoring formula.

Don't look. Unless you are *sure* that your child or someone else is in danger of imminent harm, do not divert your focus to make eye contact with what your child is doing. Think to yourself, "I see nothing, I see nothing, I see nothing." If your child is brazen enough to wave hands in front of you, or poke or prod you in some way, with as little effort as possible firmly move aside or move your child aside, but do not look at him. No glares, eye-rolling, or other facial expressions are permitted. You are to remain poker-faced throughout.

Don't discuss. This is never, never the time to argue, lecture, cajole, bribe, plead, threaten, or use any other verbal means to deal with the situation at hand. Do not answer any question, justify your rules, or repeat limitations. Do not engage with your child in any way by use of language. Any dialogue with your child when he is whining, sulking, complaining, or pleading for something will only escalate the situation. Pay no more attention to his words than you would to a screeching crow outside your window.

Don't get involved. Again, unless you see a real threat to safety, go about your previous business as best you can. Do not show any body language or gestures (e.g., sighs, hands in the air) that give your child the impression that she has you on a leash. Nothing means nothing—no attention of any kind is what extinguishes the flames.

Don't reengage. This is a vital part of ignoring. Children who do not get the attention or response they want right away often try to reengage a little later. If you are home or in a safe place where you can depart from the immediate place where your child is misbehaving, do so. Turning your back on the tantrum shows your child that you are not going to get sucked into the drama. And if you are not a player, they will eventually realize it is not working. For example, Nina asks permission to use the phone to call friends, but you have said "no" since she has not yet done the dishes or finished her homework.

EXAMPLE OF PROPER IGNORING

NINA	MOM
"Can I use the phone to call Tricia?"	"Not until you have finished your chores."
"But, Mom. I *have* to call her right now!"	
"Mom, *pleeze!* It can't wait."	
"Oooo! I hate it when you're like this!	
"You're so *mean!*"	
"Just forget it then, and forget about the chores, too!"	
"You can just do them yourself!!!" [Nina stomps off to her room and slams the door with theatrical flair.]	

Notice that this exchange is a *one-liner* for Mom. What you can't see but can imagine is Mom sitting at the kitchen table reviewing some documents for tomorrow's work. She says her one line and nothing more. As Nina escalates, Mom maintains a stone face, does not turn around to look at her, does not bow to her demands when she pleads about the urgency of the matter, and stays disengaged all the way through. Ultimately Nina becomes frustrated, throws down what she believes to be the gauntlet by threatening to disregard her chores, and takes her leave melodramatically for effect. Mom will now be done with this and behave from here on as though it had not occurred. If Nina tries again later, Mom will remain disengaged until Nina complies with her chore obligations. If she does so correctly and within the scheduled time, Mom may allow her to make a brief call if no other rules are broken. At some later time, if it appears Nina would benefit from discussing what took place, it may be brought up. However, be careful with this and only use it if you believe your child is capable of developing useful insight. Otherwise, just let the behavioral dynamics do the teaching.

Notice what happened here, going backward from the outcome. In the end, the whining and badgering resulted in nothing, while completion of chores on time and as expected earned Nina the use of the phone. This viewpoint cannot be emphasized enough. Because the payoffs are what reinforce behaviors in children, we must not overlook the power of ignoring behaviors we want to diminish, and we must not mistakenly reinforce them with attention.

In the first column on the next page list unwanted behaviors that you intend to ignore. Leave the second column blank for now.

BEHAVIORS TO IGNORE

(behaviors you want to stop)

BEHAVIORS TO PRAISE

(behaviors you want to increase)

Praise and Behavior Boosters

While one could conceivably learn *about* parenting in advance, parenting in theory is nothing like the hands-on process. Parenting is hard work, particularly with a challenging child or children who tend to wear us out. In fact, research has demonstrated that while more than 90 percent of parents think parenting is the most important thing they do, 88 percent also find the day-in and day-out experience of it as fairly to extremely stressful. We could reasonably assume the parents of difficult temperament kids fall into the "extremely stressed" group.

Think about these statistics from both the parent and the child's perspective: The average parent hears more than 20,000 words a day from their child *by the time a child is three years old!* Parents of difficult school-age children give up to sixty instructions per hour and often say "no" as frequently as eight times per hour! If the primary message a problematical child hears is "no," or "stop that," or some other complaint from a parent or teacher, that is what they will get used to and come to expect. When negative feedback from others is what happens most of the time, self-esteem plummets and any hope the child may have to do things better goes down with it.

With the most difficult child, we must work hard to not let interactions be all negative all the time. The positive part of selective attention is just as important as ignoring or disciplining with privilege removal. Yes, it's true, parents who deal with difficult-temperament children have a hard time with positive attention because there seems to be so many more instances when they child needs correcting or redirection. Nevertheless, if we want to increase a particular desirable behavior in a child we must do more. To turn bad behavior into good, it is necessary to regularly "catch" good behavior and reinforce it with positive attention.

Positive attention comes in many forms and is easy to deliver. Here are some forms of positive attention that reinforce good behaviors: smiles, nodding, pats on the back, hugs, verbal praise with lots of enthusiasm, clapping, pointing out the good behavior to someone else, stars on a chart, beans in a jar, paper tickets (the carnival type that comes on a roll), tokens, stickers, and so forth. Rather than ignore or simply expect good behavior and take it for granted when it happens, while in the process of reshaping bad behavior into good we must pay much attention when a child behaves as we wish. Positive reinforcement is the glue that will keep the new, wanted behavior in place while the ignored, unwanted behavior fades. Of course, we will not praise these behaviors every time they occur because eventually they will become habits, and excessive praise would be overkill. However, it is useful to praise the continuation of desirable behaviors randomly to be sure that as children grow they know their constructive acts and cooperative attitude are noticed and appreciated.

The easiest way to plan your reinforcement strategy is to couple behaviors you want to stop (by ignoring) with an opposing behavior that you want to increase (by praising). Go back to the two columns above and write a desirable behavior that you want to see from your child instead of the one you plan to ignore. They must be written in words that clearly describe behavior. This may not be as easy as the list of unwanted behaviors, so here are some examples of unwanted and wanted behaviors that are paired together as opposites.

BEN'S BEHAVIORS TO IGNORE (behaviors you want to stop)	BEN'S BEHAVIORS TO PRAISE (behaviors you want to increase)
1. Whines when he wants something	1. Asks nicely with a soft tone and "please"
2. Interrupts others in conversations	2. Let's others finish; says "excuse me"
3. Grabs toys from other children	3. Asks politely to play with it later
4. Pushes to be first in line	4. Waits in line without touching others
5. Leaves soda cans on the counter	5. Puts cans in the recycling right away
6. Grumbles while doing chores	6. Completes chores without complaining
7. Tells his sister what to do	7. Leaves parenting to the parents
8. Does not come inside when called	8. Comes in 3 minutes after being called
9. Dirty clothes are left on bedroom floor	9. Dirty clothes in hamper by 8:00 P.M.
10. Stays in the shower too long	10. Showers in less than 10 minutes

11. Plays stereo too loud	11. Lowers volume immediately when asked

When you have completed both columns, check to be sure they are written in such plain language that anyone coming to visit you could easily know which behaviors to ignore and which to praise. You will also be better prepared to act according to your plan, and not simply react as you have in the past, if you mentally rehearse each of these. Take them one at a time, starting with what you intend to ignore. Visualize yourself holding your ground and following the Ignore Formula to the letter—you don't look at your child's behavior, you don't say anything to him about it or to anyone else, and you maintain an expressionless poker face. For the opposite response when your child behaves well, see yourself looking at your child with a pleased and glad expression, and imagine how else you will congratulate your child's efforts, emphasizing that he or she did it (e.g., "Shaine, that was absolutely fantastic! You asked to go over to play with Nick so politely and nicely and you even said 'please.' I am so proud of you! That was very grown up!"—followed by a pat on the back or hug).

STEP # 2

ACKNOWLEDGE WANTED BEHAVIORS

Do smile. Do praise.

Do appreciate. Do hug.

Most unwanted behaviors can be positively influenced by the proper and timely application of selective attention. Ignoring and praise are highly influential parenting strategies that you cannot afford to be without. However, disobedience and disregard for family rules and expectations should never be ignored. Those transgressions are taken care of by the privileges "on" and "off" system. By applying both privilege management and selective attention you stand a very, very good chance of improving your child's behaviors in short order.

Don't forget, children thrive on positive attentions and need to feel loved and appreciated. Parents of difficult-temperament kids, or parents who were raised in an atmosphere of negativity and criticism, are often in the habit of using disapproving and correcting words more often than any other. Unfortunately, negative talk is detrimental and undermines the effectiveness of your parenting plan. Besides, it just doesn't work. All children need positive encouragement and appreciation. Yet research has shown that children with difficult temperaments need more positive feedback and encouragement than other children, though in reality their behavior often elicits more negatives and very few positives from adults than do their peers. The following is a list of words of praise and encouragement that may come in handy. Remember to pair them with smiles and enthusiastic gestures:

Good for you. That's the way to do it. Correct. Very good. That's right. Nice work. I'm so pleased with how you behaved. Great going. Wonderful. You made such a good choice there. Excellent. That's bet-

ter.   Great job.   I like the way you _____ .
Good job remembering.   You are great at that.   You
are improving your _____ more and more.   I
like that.   Terrific.   You did _____ without
needing to be reminded.   I am sure glad that you are my
son/daughter.   Now you've got it.   Way to go.   I noticed how well you controlled yourself there.   You did
such a fine job of _____ .   Keep it up.   What
a great idea.   I appreciate the way you _____ .
You showed such grown-up behavior when you
_____ .   It was so kind of you to
_____ .   You really helped a lot.   You can do it
all on your own now.   I love you!

How and When to Use
Incentives and Rewards

Many parents ask me about using special rewards as an incentive for better behavior. I believe they should be used very
carefully and not very often. Far too many parents get caught
in the trap of bribing their children to behave well. Consequently, children learn that no one should expect good behavior from them unless they pay for it. It is probably best to stick
with the basics of privilege management and selective attention until you really believe your child is under far better self-
control.

Once you have had success bringing about better behavior,
under certain conditions the use of incentives and rewards can

be quite beneficial. Rewards are especially useful for developing behaviors and habits that require preplanning, organizing, prioritizing, and delaying satisfaction. For instance, if you would like your child to learn to save money, plan ahead to get all the necessary materials ready and complete a long-term project on time, or earn behavior points toward a desired goal (new video game, day at the ball game with Dad, trip to the zoo, slumber party, dollhouse, afternoon at the park). Then help him keep track of his stepwise progress so he can feel encouraged and hopeful along the way. Let him know that you notice his patience and perseverance, and how much closer he is to achieving his reward. Help him visualize the day he earns his big payoff and how proud he will be to have done it on his own. Also, reinforce how grown-up this behavior is, and how it will serve him well in the future.

As children grow older self-management for the completion of tasks becomes more and more important, especially at school. Parents can help prepare their children to be proactive self-starters at home by supplying material rewards along with praise. The need to provide material rewards will diminish over time as youngsters develop a sense of self-respect and gain the internal reward of satisfaction for jobs well done. The internal sense of accomplishment will increase and sometimes supplant the value of external rewards (good grades, awards, or other recognitions) and contribute over time to their self-esteem.

Should your child be ready for incentives, be sure the following are part of your program:

√ The overall outcome is very important (e.g., better grades, stay out of school detention, money for a special trip to the amusement park, new basketball shoes).

√ The motivating reward is something the child really desires—enough so that he or she will want to work for it.

√ The reward is affordable, and it is achievable in a reasonable amount of time with a reasonable amount of success.

√ Reward progress is tracked to increase incentive along the way—success inspires success.

√ The reward is tied directly to the desired, very specific, behavioral goal.

√ The behavioral goal *may* already be addressed in another way (use of privilege removal as a consequence for noncompliance as well as application of selective attention), and the reward is intended to spur on even better effort.

Let me give you an example of an incentive plan that worked well. A family I worked with recently decided it was time to use an incentive with their daughter, Tara. They had been following the *Dr. J Way* protocols for several months and Tara's behavior was much better. They were no longer struggling every day with tantrums, demands, and refusal to cooperate. They were very pleased with Tara's progress, but wanted Tara to become more self-reliant about her homework. Her teachers saw improvement in Tara's behaviors at school as well, but they continued to report to her parents that she often fell behind in her assignments because she was so disorganized. It seemed to them that Tara wanted to do her work on time, but she was hindered because she didn't seem to have any consistent method of keeping track of her assignments or when projects were due.

Tara's one and only way to stay on top of her assignments was to rely on her memory. Tara was chronically forgetful. She was repeatedly surprised and disappointed in herself when asked to turn in assignments she had either left at home or forgotten entirely. Her parents knew forgetting assignments was not going to serve her well as her school career went forward, and decided this was a problem that needed to be addressed.

Because Tara was quite a resourceful and creative girl, we decided it might be best if she were to do some research on her own behalf. She was to come up with two or three new ways to keep track of her assignments, due dates, and upcoming projects or tests, using no more than fifteen dollars' worth of materials. Her motivation to do the research and select a plan for keeping track of assignments would depend upon the possibility of earning a privilege important to her. I told Tara's parents that it would be a mistake to assume they already knew the best motivator to bring about the desired effect—Tara was the only one who would know. They sat down with Tara after dinner and asked her to list some things that they might be able to provide that would please her very much in return for changing her behavior. They wanted to know what would motivate her enough to make and stick with a plan for keeping track of her school assignments. To their surprise she answered gleefully, "I know exactly what it is! I have been dying to learn how to ride a horse!" Had Tara's parents not asked they may have never known that Tara was harboring this burning desire. They would have guessed she would prefer a slumber party, new clothes, or a new bike. Tara's parents were pleased to discover there was a stable not too far away from her grandparents' house that offered riding lessons at a reasonable price.

Now it was Tara's turn to do the investigating. She spent some time asking friends she knew to be highly organized what they did to stay on top of homework. Then she explored some online suggestions at homework sites for kids. Lastly, she asked her dad to take her to a store that sold planners and organizers. At first she tried to convince her parents that the very best plan of all would be the purchase of a handheld computer/organizer. But knowing Tara as well as they did, her parents quickly foresaw this as a lost item before they even paid the credit card bill. So, much to Tara's chagrin, that idea had to be scrapped. Her parents were willing to spend up to fifteen dollars on whatever materials she needed to get schoolwork organized.

Eventually Tara settled on a plan that combined the use of three things: (1) an assignment book for keeping track of daily homework, (2) a monthly calendar on her dresser mirror so she could see at a glance what was coming up (like tests, projects, permission slips for field trips, and so on, marking days with a star when she should start to get ready), and (3) photocopies of a checklist for her backpack that she would complete every night before bed, placing her backpack by the door. Once her parents understood her plan, they helped Tara create and copy the backpack checklist. Tara also decided to enlist the help of one of her highly organized friends as a backup person, while they rode the bus home together, to make sure she had down all the assignments and due dates. Tara's parents discussed the plan with her teachers, who agreed to report back to them every Friday for the next several weeks about how Tara was doing with her assignments.

Rather than emphasize times when Tara slipped up, she and her parents agreed on a record-keeping plan that highlighted her successes. To create a visual reminder of the incentive, Tara used a few dollars that weren't spent on her organizing materials to buy a large picture of a beautiful horse. She and her parents posted the print on her bedroom wall. Tara then cut printer paper into strips and taped them together to make what looked like a long and winding sidewalk that had thirty stepping stones in it. Her parents had promised her that when her teachers had reported thirty days of completing all her assignments on time, she would earn the riding lessons she longed for. As a further incentive, the following weekend when the family was on the way to visit Tara's grandparents, they made a stop at the stables to meet with Tara's prospective riding teacher. Tara was enthralled—what had been a pipe dream started to look like a real possibility, and achieving it depended on her. Sure enough, in about forty days (most successes are not instantaneous, no matter how motivated children are to change), Tara was all grins atop Cinnamon, her newfound equine friend. She was organized, her teachers were pleased, her parents were delighted, and best of all, her self-esteem went up a notch as she acknowledged how she had turned things around at school by her own efforts, and that she had earned this wonderful reward all by herself.

All of the parental responses involving attention discussed in this chapter share the same goals: increase wanted behaviors and decrease unwanted behaviors. Correctly ignoring and offering positive attention are the most important factors in behavior change, because they are the primary tools parents have at their disposal that either reinforce a behavior or serve to extinguish it. Incentives and rewards are sometimes helpful, especially for children who are highly motivated to work for something they really want. Reward systems should be well-thought-out and used on occasion so your child doesn't get the mistaken idea that you have to "buy" his or her good behavior. Remember also to continue to randomly praise and acknowledge your child's good behaviors to keep them going and to support the development of healthy self-esteem.

[10]

Consistency Is Key: Don't Get Creative

In real estate it's *location, location, location* that matters. In parenting, *consistency, consistency, consistency* means everything. If you are going to take your new plan seriously you must commit yourself to being consistent. This will not be easy. Your child will try again and again to throw you off track, hoping you will go back to your old ways. While it might become a little boring to use the same plan over and over it will be well worth it. In fact, the closer you toe the line, the better your results, so don't get creative to shake things up—stick with the program.

The military is so highly disciplined because the rules are anything but flimsy and unpredictable. While you are not going to run a home-based boot camp, you do need to hold your ground and stick very tightly to the rules about ignoring and paying attention. Parents usually get tripped up when they take the bait to argue or justify or lecture, when in fact the less said the better. If your expectations and rules are reasonable and clear-cut, and if you know your child understands the rules and consequences, you will have nothing to explain or repeat. The only time you would ever repeat a rules or expectation is if you honestly believe your child does not understand, though I find this is rarely the case. In the face of whatever your child does, remain calm, succinct, and determined. You will not be drawn into arguments that make you look foolish or be tempted to say things you will later regret. You have laid out a plan and you will not deviate from it. Even if you are boiling on the inside, you will present a calm, self-assured demeanor at all times. That is how you stay in charge.

Take some time to think about your own personality, habits, apprehensions, and stress level. Try to anticipate situations that will make you vulnerable to backing down and not enforcing the rules. Challenging and stressful situations will occur, so it is important to be at the ready. Will you be vulnerable to caving in at certain times of the day? Are you at risk when you feel tired or angry about something that happened at work? Will you lose it if you don't feel well? Will the plan be in jeopardy if you need support from someone else for a short time, but you don't get it? Will it be a challenge to follow through if you feel anxious or overwhelmed? Will you be tempted to abandon the plan when you are busy trying to get something important done and you don't want to take time to deal with your child's behavior problems?

All parents become stressed and overwhelmed at times. It is especially difficult for single parents and those with insufficient support networks. Consider developing a supportive partnership with a friend or neighbor so when things get rocky you can call each other and offer some words of support and encouragement. Look for ways to take time-outs by arranging for a sitter or relative to take over for an hour or two a week. Plan some fun things that you know will go well for you and your child, to add some positive interactions during the week. Try creating a "quiet time" each evening when you each sit in the same room, but do something individual that is calm (e.g., your child colors in a coloring book while you read a novel).

If you are in a two-parent family it will be helpful to use a tag-team approach. Discuss with your parenting partner situations you have identified for each of you when you are at risk of becoming inconsistent and letting your plan fall apart. Solve problems together and develop signals that you can give to each other that indicate when you are reaching your breaking point, at which time you hand off the behavior management to your partner for a while. This will give each of you breaks, and also provides opportunities to present a united front. Your child's trust level will also increase when he or she recognizes that both of you are on the same page with your expectations and that you are equally capable of giving consequences and praise.

Charting Progress Keeps Things Going

One of the best ways to stay on course is to keep track of how things are going. Charting your child's progress will help everyone focus on the target behaviors, and your child will know that you are paying attention to his or her efforts. It is also a powerful way to encourage continued progress. Success breeds more success, and children love to participate in the process. Children need to see that their attempts to change their behavior are valued, and they will also have a visual reference (especially when there are setbacks) that they are getting somewhere. They can also show grandparents, babysitters, and others how much they have improved, which will give them a sense of pride and accomplishment.

There are many ways to chart progress that emphasize positive behaviors. Many children enjoy making a chart of their own. For younger children, a type of chart that is often appealing is similar to a board game, though in this case each step along the road is a positive step to success. Stars or stickers can be used to track progress on a very simple chart based on a calendar. Each time your child performs a target behavior well a star of sticker is added to that day. Here is one example of a very simple chart:

KYLE'S WINNING BEHAVIORS	MON	TUE	WED	THU	FRI	SAT	SUN
Gets to the bus on time	★		★	★		N/A	N/A
Clears table without being reminded		★	★		★	★	
Feeds and walks the dog before dinner without complaining or being reminded	★		★		★		★

Encourage your child by making a big deal about successes and minimizing discussion about days that were less successful. Let your child know that progress is a step-by-step process and that although you expect improvement, you do not expect perfection.

Children who love numbers and like to count things often prefer a point system (e.g., five points for each task completed as expected and on time, and twenty-five points earns a trip to the park), although for the most part this should be treated as a measurement of progress and not an automatic setup for some prize when success is achieved. In general you want your child to learn that the joy of improving and succeeding is its own reward. Be sure you show enthusiasm about charting your child's behavioral improvements, even if your child does not.

If your child is totally against keeping a chart, then you can develop one for yourself and provide your child with praise and encouragement based on your data. Remember, when your child performs behaviors that you want to reinforce, much attention and wholehearted praise should follow. If you pay no attention to your child's progress—even if it takes quite a while and your child makes only small gains—you will derail your plan and your child will become discouraged and disinterested.

When your child asks for a star or announces that he or she has earned points and you know better, rather than pointing out all the things that were done wrong that failed to earn your child a star or points, remind your child that he or she has done it well before, and/or that the current behavior did not meet with your established expectations. If it truly seems that your child is confused about what you expect, you may need to show the child exactly what you want (if it is a chore or respectful talk, for instance), or give verbal examples. Have your child explain back to you what is expected in terms of what it would look like, sound like, or act like if they did it right. Unless your expectation is very complex and requires multiple steps, you should never have to reexplain it more than once.

For young children and/or children who are very visual, it is often a good idea to have a series of instruction cards available so they can see for themselves exactly how to perform certain tasks without you needing to get involved—the less your child needs to engage you in the process the better. Here is an example of an instruction card that is young-child friendly and visually appealing:

BREANNA

**At 8:30 [picture of a moon in the night sky here]
get ready for [picture of bed here]**

- ☑ [Picture of child brushing teeth here]
- ☑ [Picture of child washing face here]
- ☑ [Picture of child dressed in pajamas here]
- ☑ [Picture of child being read a bedtime story here]
- ☑ [Picture of child sleeping here]

For older children who are expected to complete more complicated tasks, I recommend a large recipe card with the step-by-step instructions laid out in very plain and detailed language. Here is an example of an instruction card for a child who can be appropriately expected to perform a multistep task:

HOW TO CORRECTLY CLEAN MY ROOM

1. Make sure all dirty clothes are in the laundry basket or hamper and none is on the floor or hung over furniture or piled in the closet.

2. Remove bedding. Wash, dry, and replace sheets and make the bed so the bedspread is placed evenly on top and is mostly smoothed out with pillows tucked under the top.

3. Put all toys, games, books, and other loose items in drawers or on the shelves where they belong when not in use.

4. Return any food items to the kitchen; wash and put away any dishes that were in my room.

5. Dust off the furniture in my room with the treated dust cloth Mom pointed out to me.

6. Empty my wastebasket into the garbage can in the garage.

7. Vacuum the carpet, including under the desk chair and under the bed, and put the vacuum away in the back closet with the cord completely wound.

You will avoid many arguments and deter attempts by your child to make you believe he or she simply "didn't know" how to do what you expect when they can see what to do with their very own eyes. You may want to keep a few copies of these kinds of instructions in case your child "accidentally" loses it or tears it up in a fit of exasperation because they can't duck out of their obligations. However, if this happens more than once, remove all privileges and initiate the time-out system. To get out and earn back privileges, follow the usual procedure, only this time the earn-back process will also include sitting down and copying the instruction list from your master copy and then completing the task as expected.

Plug Loopholes and Make Adjustments with Care

Difficult-to-manage children are often masters at finding loopholes. So true loopholes need to be dealt with as soon as they arise. Though your child may attempt to convince you that your targeted expectations mean something other than what you have written and explained to her, her complaints and trial-lawyer tactics do not necessarily require your attention. In those cases when your child is simply trying to coerce you, do as always and ignore it entirely.

A loophole only needs to be remedied when it becomes quite clear that your expectations are incomplete, or that you had not originally taken into account certain possibilities that now face you. For instance, if your expectation for curfew states that your child is to be in the house each evening before 7:00 on weeknights and by 8:30 on weekends, this may not be a thorough enough set of standards. When your child is on school break, will the times need to be different? As the seasons change and darkness comes earlier and later, will that make a difference in what you should reasonably expect? How would your standards hold up as written if you allow your child to attend a school event that ends at 9:00?

The best defense against loopholes is a systematic review of your rules and expectations with a friend or family member to help you discover any loopholes that may need plugging. While factoring in contingencies, don't be tempted to change rules again and again or add more "for instances" ad nauseum in an effort to cover every possible scenario. The following "bottom line" rule will take care of all those times when any rule seems open to interpretation and a judgment call is required:

The Bottom Line: *"I'm the Parent and You're Not. When a Judgment Call Needs to be Made I Will Make It."*

Because circumstances can change, it is probably a good idea to evaluate the whole plan every few months to remind yourself of why you need to stick with it, and to assure yourself that the entire family is following the general family policies. After all, we cannot expect our children to behave well when we model bad behaviors ourselves. However, make changes to your behavior plan very judiciously. For your plan to work, it probably needs to be in operation at least three to four weeks, so don't rush to make changes prematurely. Because consistency is paramount, try to go all five weeks before you adjust your expectations in any way. Eventually, as your child's target behaviors improve and you believe enough time without problems has gone by, you may choose to target a different behavior.

If your child is one who is highly motivated to alter his or her behavior to earn a special reward, you may do so without changing the remainder of your expectations. Pair the most important target behavior with the incentive, and use only one target behavior at a time. Remember that incentives should be used sparingly. Do not make it a habit or regular part of your plan and do not let your child convince you that they should receive a special payoff on a regular basis.

As your child grows and develops, he or she will face new challenges and be expected to handle more responsibilities. The *Dr. J Way* is flexible enough so that it can be altered for all these conditions. The ultimate goal is a child who needs less and less guidance and application of very few consequences. Naturally occurring consequences will most often be enough to motivate a child to maintain their expected behavior (e.g., child didn't get a part in the school play due to failure to memorize lines; friend doesn't want to come over to play today because child was mean yesterday; child is in detention after school instead of playing outside because he didn't comply with school rules; child has to use his own savings to take a taxi to school because he goofed around in the morning and missed the bus; child was hungry all day because he left his lunch sitting on the kitchen table; child sits in the school office instead of accompanying her class on a field trip because she didn't turn in the permission slip).

[11]

Troubleshooting

If you have started your plan and are running into trouble, it may be helpful to review some of the guidelines. Start by going over the *Dr. J Way* steps and be sure that your behavioral expectations are (a) age-appropriate, (b) clearly laid out and understood, and (c) you are following the rules of selective attention outlined in Chapter 9.

The *Dr. J Way* Guidelines

STEP # 1: GIVE NO-NONSENSE REQUESTS AND COMMANDS

STEP # 2: TWO STRIKES AND YOUR CHILD IS OUT

STEP # 3: DULL AND DREARY DETENTION: TIME-OUT IS *NOT* ABOUT TIME

STEP # 4: OWNING THE PROBLEM: WHY YOUR CHILD NEEDS TO EXPLAIN WHAT HE/SHE DID WRONG

STEP # 5: RESTORING PRIVILEGES: THE FOUR *EARN-BACK* TASKS

1. I will calm myself down and stay calm in my time-out place for at least ten minutes. When that is done I may politely ask to come out to earn my privileges back.

2. If my parent agrees that I am ready, I will apologize *nicely*. Then I will say exactly *what* I did wrong, *why* it is wrong, and what I should have done that would not have broken a rule.

3. If I am in time-out because I didn't finish a chore on time, or if it wasn't done correctly, I will do the chore right away and do it well so my parent approves. If I am in time-out because I said or did something else that broke the rules (such as: name-calling, hitting, screaming, throwing things, taking things that don't belong to me, dawdling and missing the school bus), if someone's feeling were hurt or I made trouble for someone else, I will nicely tell the person I am sorry. Then I will write a paragraph or give a short speech to my parent about what I could have done that would have been better.

4. To "earn-back" my privileges I will complete an extra chore my parent assigns, and I will do it properly and with a good attitude.

AT ALL TIMES PARENTS MUST:

- Ignore unwanted behaviors: No looking at it, talking about it, or gesturing.
- Give much attention and praise to wanted Behaviors with smiles, hugs, congratulations, and positive-feedback words and gestures.
- Chart progress.
- Use incentives and rewards sparingly.
- Be consistent, consistent, consistent!

There are other specific areas of concern for many parents, and I have provided a group of suggestions that may be helpful to you if these issues apply in your situation. The first of these has to do with homework. For many parents the most stressful time of day is trying to get their child to sit down and do homework. Regardless of whether or not completing homework is an issue for your child, the following may help diminish the battles:

AVOIDING HOMEWORK WARS

- Use your leverage to make homework completion a routine every day that is directly tied to privileges being "on" or "off." Remember, during time-out, the only thing your child is allowed to do is unfinished homework.

■ If homework is a big problem, consider adding an incentive that your child *really* wants and is willing to earn with points for finished homework that is done without a battle.

■ Let your child face the natural consequences, and lay the responsibility for what happens at school and on the report card squarely on him.

■ Try to determine what is in the way of your child getting her homework done in a timely manner. Try to find a good time to help your child find the source of the problem and then decide who needs to do something about it. If the homework isn't being done because your child doesn't understand it, you may need to hire a tutor or request special help from the school. You may need to dig deeper to uncover the causes. Does your child:

> Procrastinate too long and run short of time?
> Forget the assignment?
> Not pay close enough attention in class to know what to do?
> Fail to gather the materials needed for a project and not have time to get them?
> Expect perfection every time and dwell on tasks, making them overly complicated and time-consuming?
> Dislike doing tasks by himself?

Complete her homework in record time and turn it in, only to be required by her teacher to do it over because it was so sloppy or inadequate?

Truly not grasp important concepts or not understand how to proceed?

Once you have a better grasp of the root of the problem you can begin to work at solutions that address your child's particular situation.

- Set up a consistent homework time and place that is conducive to study and work.
- Help children break down homework tasks into chunks and don't focus on their frustrations.
- Let your child know that you have confidence in his ability to work through his assignments.
- Make sure your child has adequate supplies to complete homework tasks. Help her go over assignments that are coming up in the future and encourage her to plan ahead if she needs to be taken to the library or a store to buy materials or make copies.

TALKING WITH AND LISTENING TO YOUR CHILD

Sometimes parents have not developed a pattern of good communication with their child, which can slow progress down. To open the lines of communication with your child, listening can be more important than what you have to say. Be sure to use your words wisely following these guidelines:

- Don't always tower over your child. Sit down together so you are at about the same level.
- Respectfully listen to your child's point of view so long as he or she maintains self-control and does not break family rules. Don't interrupt.
- Validate your child's feelings—how he or she feels is never wrong.
- Don't rush in to correct your child's thinking or solve the problem for her.
- Do not lecture, preach, or moralize.
- Don't jump in and take over when your child is telling a story or describing an event.
- Avoid answering the phone when your child is in the middle of telling you something important.
- When your child comes to you to talk and is doing so respectfully and at an appropriate time, turn off the TV and put down what you are doing to give your child your undivided attention.
- Don't attempt to communicate with your child when you are very tired or angry. Wait until you are calmer and it is less likely you will make the situation worse.
- Never trap a child who has done something wrong by asking him if he did it when you know all along he did. Simply announce what you know to be true and apply the consequences.

- Avoid asking your child, "Why did you do that?" It is nearly always irrelevant and very likely that he or she has no idea "why." Focus on what occurred without investigating the "why."

Help Your Child Learn to Reason and Solve Problems

Many parents think the best way to teach their children is by lecture. Rather than simply talking at your child in an effort to "get through" to him or her, try doing problem-solving training in more creative ways, such as making up stories with problems characters solve well and solve badly. Work out a problem sequence on paper like a board game ("what would be the next smart move?"), or go over past events and choices of action and see what other options may have been overlooked and discuss possible outcomes. You can help older children develop their ability to anticipate consequences with a form of bubble chart. Draw a circle with a problem in it (e.g., missed the school bus). Then have your child draw three or four lines from the problem bubble and add a circle on the end of each. Ask her to think of a possible solution and write it in each bubble. Then draw another line that extends each of these options to an outcome bubble. Have her tell you which is the best and which would be the worst choice, given what she has drawn out. At first your child may need your help to come up with optional choices of action, but soon she will be able to add this reasoning tool to her problem-solving skills, if you make it fun and reward her with praise for her good thinking.

It is also useful to help your child identify things that are

beyond her control (e.g., it rains on her birthday party and a pic-
nic at the park was planned) and find ways to flexibly adjust or
let go of what can't be fixed or undone. And remember to take
your child's experiences seriously. Don't rush to dismiss as trivial
what is important to your child (e.g., "Worse things have happened"; "You'll get over it"; or, "Well, what did you expect?").
Show your child that you are accepting of him, regardless of
what he has done or not done, and keep the doors of communication open by reflecting back what they seem to be feeling
more than anything else (e.g., "Sounds like you had a tough
day"; "You seem so sad about that"; "Looks to me like you're
pretty worried"; "You are so pleased to have earned that A").

Teach Your Child How to Express Angry Feelings

For many difficult-temperament children, anger is an issue
that needs to be addressed. Many such children engage in in-
appropriate expressions of anger—yelling, hitting, throwing
toys, and so on. The following strategies may help to defuse a
future blowup:

- Angry feelings are okay, but people, animals, and
  things are not to be hurt.
- Stop and take three deep breaths and sigh them out
  very slowly, as if you were trying to blow a feather
  clear across the room.
- Try to decide if this upset would go in the Big Deal
  box or the Little Deal box, so your child will learn

to match emotional reactions appropriately, depending on the seriousness of the situation (e.g., losing a hair ribbon would go in the Little Deal box, while losing a pet would go in the Big Deal box). It is important for children to learn that hurts and disappointments come in all sizes and to develop a variety of emotional reactions to avoid interpreting every little stumbling block as a disaster and overreacting.

- Think of five ways you could react to what happened without hurting anyone or anything.
- Use words that don't hurt to work out your anger ("That makes me really mad"; "I don't like it when you _____"; "I am so angry that that happened").
- Draw your angry feelings on paper.
- Shake your anger out or go outside and stomp it into the sidewalk—don't bottle it up inside of you.
- When you are calmer, talk over what happened with someone you trust; look for ideas of how to handle situations like this one.
- Remind yourself that you don't always get to have your way, and that you don't have to get upset about little things.
- Congratulate yourself when you have calmed down and dealt with angry feelings responsibly.
- Help your child keep track of times when she manages her anger well and offer praise.

Raising a Child with ADHD/ADD

Children with attention deficit hyperactivity disorder—ADHD/ADD—nearly always fall into the "difficult temperament" group. They are often in a state of perpetual motion and activity. Because they have an attention deficit that is part of their wiring, they fail to take notice of or have trouble understanding important directions. Here are some things you can do to help:

Set up house rules. Make the rules of behavior for the family simple, clear, and short. Rules should be explained clearly. It's important to explain what will happen when the rules are obeyed and when they are broken. Write down the rules and results of not following them and post it where they can have easy access to it. The punishment for breaking rules should be fair, quick, and consistent.

Use positive "what to do" language. The most common form of interaction children with ADHD experience is being told what they are doing wrong. Tell your child what you want him to do so he knows what is expected, and not just what you don't want. Make every effort to engage in selective attention—praise little things like closing the door without slamming it. Children with ADHD need to be praised for good behavior more than their peers, so catching them doing things right should be part of your daily plan.

Set up a home schedule and stick to routines. Many things during your child's day need to be structured. Because the ADHD mind is not one to be organized or to prioritize or prefer structure, you will need to put these in place. Some daily events that can be scheduled into a routine include: specific times to get up in the morning, meal times, play time, homework, doing chores, talking on the phone, watching TV or playing video games, bathing, and bedtime. Have your child help you write out his or her schedule and post it where everyone can see it. For young children or those with reading difficulties, include drawings or magazine photos, or create symbols as a kind of shorthand that can quickly remind your child what they need to do or what to do next. When changes in your schedule need to be made, try to take the time to explain the reasons to your child. It is helpful to explain any changes in routine in advance and make sure your child understands the changes.

When you give your child an instruction or command, be sure that your child "gets it." Do not yell to your child from the next room or expect him to pay attention to you if he is busy doing something. Ask your child to come to where you are, or go to where she is. For young children, gently take your child's hands and hold them while you make sure they are giving you their eye contact. For older children, turn off the TV or computer or whatever has them engaged, to let them know you expect their full attention. Keep directions simple and short. Tell your child in a firm and calm voice exactly what you want her to do. Ask your child to repeat it back to you. For tasks that require several steps, give one or two instructions at a time, or with older children write out in bullet points what to do, in what order, and precisely how to do it. Try not to turn into a living reminder service. If you know that your child has heard and understood your instructions and does not comply right away after two requests, your child should be sent to time-out immediately and continue with the privileges "on," privileges "off" method.

Be consistent. Be realistic in your expectations and demands. Don't threaten or promise what you can't or probably won't deliver. ADHD children need to learn that you mean what you say and that you are going to do what you say you will do. If you have a schedule, make every effort to stick with it. If you have family rules, don't abandon them in the face of your child's challenging behaviors. Parents of ADHD children need to maintain a steady-as-you-go model, no matter how disorganized and unruly their children are.

Provide the appropriate level of supervision. Because the majority of ADHD children are impulsive, it stands to reason that they need more adult supervision than other children their age. Young ADHD children should not spend much time out of view of a concerned adult. Make sure your child is supervised by adults all day. Although you don't want to hound your child or overmonitor him, letting him have too much freedom too soon can spell disaster. Inform other adults and caregivers who regularly spend time with your child about his ADHD situation and ask that they pay close attention to what is going on when you are not there. Consult with teachers, online professional support organizations, or child mental health specialists whenever you feel you need to better understand your child and learn more about what might be done to help your child learn. Become a lay expert in ADHD and learn how to advocate for your child. Find materials you can share with your child so he can understand himself better. Consider joining a support group for parents of ADHD children, some of which are provided in the Resources section on page 193.

Help your ADHD child learn social skills. It's hard for children with ADHD to learn social skills and to follow accepted rules of social behavior. Try to help your child choose playmates with similar developmental skills. Many ADHD children do best when they play with only one or two other children at a time. Praise your child when she takes turns nicely, plays by the rules, doesn't boss other children, shares, and is polite to others. Never allow hitting, pushing, and yelling in your house or yard. Help your child to develop self-esteem and to learn to compete with herself more than with others.

Get ready for school the night before. School mornings may be difficult for children with ADHD. Select school clothes and put them out. Have your child prepare his backpack and go over a checklist to be sure everything he will need for school has been included. Place the backpack by the door. If your child carries a lunch to school, make it together and put it in the refrigerator. Post a "Did you remember?" list on the back of the door through which he will leave and make sure he goes over it carefully. Recognize your child's pace and wake your child early enough to allow adequate time to get dressed, eat breakfast, and brush teeth without getting frenzied.

Focus on progress, not perfection. Remember that your ADHD child is wired in such a way as to make many seemingly ordinary tasks difficult. That doesn't mean you shouldn't have standards or expect improvement. But effort matters. Notice and praise your child when she tries hard to do her schoolwork well, not just for getting good grades. Help your child give herself credit for doing better with a charting system that shows only good behaviors. Show your child that you value education and reading, and read enjoyable stories together because research is clear that when parents place importance on learning and reading their children do better in school. Encourage your child to ask questions, discuss stories, tell the story to someone else, and to reread stories to younger children. Take your child to the library regularly (many libraries have book reading events that children enjoy) and encourage him to select books of interest, and later share what he has read with you. Provide stimulating books and reading material around the house. Foster concentration by reducing distracting features of your child's environment as much as possible. Teach your child ways to compensate for any learning limitations or disabilities.

Concerns About Sensory
Integration Problems

In Chapter 1 we explored issues of temperament related to problem behaviors in children. A small number of difficult-temperament children have diagnosable problems or delays with sensory integration that may require the services of an occupational therapist. Sensory integrative dysfunction is a processing problem in the brain that causes the incorporation of sensory system information to be inefficient, and the interpretation of sensory input may be incorrect. For most people, our senses (smell, touch, hearing, vision, taste) and our movements work together to provide us with an organized and accurate awareness of where we are, who we are, and what is happening around us. This ability begins to develop early in life as children grow and their brains mature. When this happens normally, children don't need to pay much attention to or spend effort on motor movements and adjusting to various sensations in order to function well.

Children with sensory integrative dysfunction may seem as intelligent as their peers, though they may have difficulty playing with certain toys, brushing their hair or getting dressed, or manipulating a pencil. Sometimes they seem to be overly cautious around swing sets or other playground equipment, because they don't trust their physical coordination. Some of these children are just the opposite and seem to be reckless and overly active.

If you have a young child who shows a number of the following symptoms, he or she may have sensory integrative dysfunction:

Highly sensitive to touch, movement, bright lights and sights, or certain sounds (or shows a lack of expected reaction to touch, sights, or sounds).

Displays social problems one wouldn't expect from a child that age.

Often seems careless and clumsy.

Is hyperactive or underactive.

Becomes upset when required to stop what he or she is doing, or when the situation changes.

Is highly distractible and skips from one thing to another far more than you would expect from a child that age.

Cannot self-calm when excited or upset.

Has poor self-concept.

Has poor self-regulation and is frequently out of control.

Is overly emotional, and reactions to ordinary events often seem out of proportion.

Displays delays in speech, language, motor skills, and/or learning.

Steps can be taken to help a child who may have a sensory integrative disorder. An evaluation by a certified occupational or physical therapist is often a good place to start. The professional evaluation may include standardized tests and observations of responses to sensory stimulation, posture, balance, coordination, and eye movements. Parents will usually provide a good deal of information about their child, and together with the therapist's recommendations they will determine the appropriate treatment. Treatment includes a variety of techniques to help the child respond more effectively to sensory input and to develop new skills for improved motor movement and coordination, self-calming, and so forth. Resources are provided on page 193.

When Other Services May Be Needed

Though I do not recommend as a first step, or even a necessary step, an evaluation for medication to address difficult temperament or behavior problems, there are some cases where medication may be a wise thing to consider. For children with multiple problems (e.g., ADHD and a learning disability; sensory integration dysfunction and high family stress) who do not seem to respond to serious efforts to help them change their behaviors, the appropriate medication may help the child to be less reactive or impulsive long enough to make changes possible. If you reach the point where you can honestly say that you have consistently applied the *Dr. J Way* plan for at least five weeks as laid out in this book, and there are no new situations or stressors that would explain why your child's behavior is not improving, you may want to consult with a child psychiatrist, child development specialist, or your pediatrician. The best decision about whether or not to use medication in your particular case is likely to be made when you have become well informed about your child's specific temperamental style, behavior patterns, stressors in the family and at school, and other factors that may lead to a diagnosis that would lend itself to medication.

You know your child better than anyone else, and you are the person in the best position to advocate for your child. At the same time the responsibility to really understand your child's temperament, strengths, and weaknesses fall to you. As parents, when you are well informed you will be better prepared to speak to professionals plainly about the concerns you have about your child's behavior, what you want and need for your child, and what types of help you are seeking. Remember, the final say about medications or no medication is always yours.

[Appendix A]

Tips for Managing Difficult-Temperament Types

HIGH ACTIVITY LEVEL

- Become aware of signals that your child is becoming overstimulated or worked up, and help him/her find a way to blow off steam and calm down so self-control can be regained. One good way is to have your child go to a quiet spot and separate colored beans, cotton balls, or ribbons in plastic bowls. This rhythmic activity allows the overcharged midbrain that is causing all the fuss and emotional overload to slow down and return to a normal pace. The child's hands, eyes, and thoughts are just busy enough with this mundane task to keep them engaged. After a short time the child will look and feel calmer. Be sure you point out this positive change in your child and congratulate him for calming down all by himself. Then let him know that because he did such a good job of self-calming he is now ready to go back to his activities and be with others.
- Try to incorporate some high energy–active times each day.

■ When confinement (time-out) is used, be sure to provide your child with self-calming materials that are ready to go, and remind them that if and when they are in time-out they will get out sooner if they perform one or more of these activities.

SLOW TO ADAPT

■ Acknowledge the stress your child experiences in new situations and encourage him or her to talk about their feelings and apprehensions.

■ Whenever possible, go to new places in advance, role-play, or practice how you expect your child to behave before going into new situations.

■ Avoid surprises as much as you can. Let your child know what is coming up and give him or her time to get used to the idea of change.

■ When appropriate, give a five- or ten-minute warning to your child when it is time to stop playing or to do something else.

HIGHLY DISTRACTIBLE

■ Keep your instructions short and clear, and always make sure you have your child's undivided attention before giving them.

■ As much as possible, maintain a calm, low-stimulation atmosphere in your home. Create a work space for your child to do homework in that has very few external distractions.

■ Play games and encourage activities that require concentration for success, and offer praise whenever your child sticks with a task despite distractions or frustrations.

■ Develop a special signal or gesture that reminds your child to get back on task.

■ When possible, plan breaks in your child's schedule, rather than allowing your child to impulsively switch gears and stop work-in-progress whenever an urge to do so arises.

INTENSE REACTIVITY

- Teach your child self-calming and self-reassuring methods (e.g., have your child separate by color a number of ribbons, beans, poker chips, or cotton balls from one large bowl to several small bowls or boxes. This type of activity is hands-on and requires just enough concentration to calm the child down. Or, if your child has a tendency to explode when frustrations build, have him sit down with legs crossed, clutch his arms around himself, lower his head, and close his eyes and count backwards from 100—older children should count backwards by fours to keep their minds occupied).

- Role-play a variety of responses to situations. Make it a game where your child rates each enactment as too big a reaction (red sign), too little reaction (yellow sign), and just right (green sign). Whenever the red sign is held up, the over-the-top actor must sit and perform a self-calming task. Ask your child to identify when you look and act as though you are calm and in control of yourself, and then put up the green sign as the go-ahead to resume activities. Then reverse the process and have your child play the parts while you put up the signs.

- Train your child in meditation, realistic self-talk, and anger management skills, or find a local professional to help your child learn these techniques.

NEGATIVE MOOD

- Generally ignore grumbling and complaining.
- Encourage your child to talk about things that are happy; start off the evening meal with everyone describing three good things about their day.
- Model a positive outlook and vocalize your awareness of beauty, pleasant things, nice people, and strokes of good luck.

POOR PERSISTENCE

- Reward your child for being persistent and finishing tasks, especially in the face of frustration or setbacks.
- Break down assignments and larger tasks into doable chunks and praise your child for each successive completion.
- Set timed work periods with small breaks built in and allow your child to engage in a rewarding event when the work is complete.

POOR PREDICTABILITY

- Establish routines. Set up expectations that involve structure: make a list of what your child is expected to do to get ready for bed and post it in the bathroom; insist that your child sit through dinner even if not hungry and go to bed on time even if not sleepy.
- Model doing certain activities consistently, whether you feel like it or not at the time (e.g., doing the dishes, exercising, walking the dog, paying bills, doing laundry) within an atmosphere that also allows for flexibility.
- Help your child learn how to keep track of his assignments, projects, and other tasks so he increasingly prompts himself to get things done.

HIGHLY SENSITIVE

- Encourage your child to dress in layers so adjustments to temperature differences can be made easily.
- Whenever possible, keep excessive stimulation to a minimum: noisy crowds, loud music, flashing lights, perfumes, and so on.
- Let your child know that you are accepting of his or her sensitivities and together explore ways to deal with them for increased comfort.

WITHDRAWAL

- Allow your child time to adjust. Don't push him or her to "jump in" right away.
- Gently encourage your child to try new things, to make new friend, and to be curious.
- Model reasonable risk-taking as well as reasonable cautiousness.

[Appendix B]

Four Steps to Get
Out of Time-out and
Earn Back Privileges

1. I will calm myself down and stay calm in my time-out place for at least ten minutes. When that is done I may politely ask to come out to earn my privileges back.
2. If my parent agrees that I am ready, I will apologize *nicely*. Then I will say exactly WHAT I did wrong, WHY it is wrong, and *what* I should have done that would not have broken a rule.
3. If I am in time-out because I didn't finish a chore on time, or if it wasn't done correctly, I will do the chore right now and do it well so my parent approves. If I am in time-out because I said or did something else that broke the rules (such as: name-calling, hitting, screaming, throwing things, taking things that don't belong to me, dawdling and missing the school bus) I will write a paragraph or give a short speech to my parent about what I could have done that would have been better. If someone's feelings were hurt or I made trouble for someone else, I will nicely tell the person I am sorry.

4. To earn back my privileges I will complete an extra chore my parent assigns, and I will do it properly and with a good attitude.

WARNING! If ANY ONE of the steps is NOT done properly, I will be returned to time-out and I will have to start over at number 1.

[Appendix C]

Sample Behavior Plan

All family members agree to use respectful talk and behavior with each other. We will use a moderate tone of voice, and will not insult others, call people names, yell, hit, kick, break things, or take other's things without their permission. We will not interrupt people when they are talking, and will ask questions and express our feelings in a respectful manner. We will all manage our own feelings and will remove ourselves to calm down when we are very upset.

Expectations for _____ (child's name)

1. **Curfew:** Unless permission is granted beforehand, _____ will be home and in the house on school days at _____ o'clock on weekends at _____ o'clock and during school vacation at _____ o'clock. A five-minute grace period may be allowed for differences in clocks and watches. It is

_____ 's responsibility to know the time or come in immediately when called.

2. **Schoolwork and school behavior:** _____ will attend
school each school day unless ill or for another reason permitted
by parent(s). _____ is expected to be at the bus corner
on time, attend all classes on time, follow the school rules, and
complete all homework as assigned and turn it in on time.
_____ will show respect to teachers and other students
and wear clothing to school that meets with the approval of par-
ent(s) and school staff. _____ will maintain grades no
lower than _____ in every class.

4. **Friends and activities:** _____ will make good decisions
about who she chooses to spend time with in and out of school.
_____ will not associate with children who break rules
or who regularly conduct themselves in ways her parent(s) would
not allow. _____ will get permission from parent(s) before leaving the house. _____ will get permission to go
out with friends, and parent(s) must approve having anyone over
to the house, and only when a parent is at home.

5. **Telephone use:** _____ will be allowed to use the phone
to call friends or receive calls from friends between the hours of
_____ and _____ on school nights and until
_____ on weekends or school vacations. Unless special
permission is granted, calls must be limited to _____
minutes. No long-distance calls may be placed without parental
permission. The time between phone conversations will be at least
_____ . No more than _____ total minutes of
phone time will be allowed on school nights. If another family
member needs to use the phone, _____ will respectfully
tell her friend she will need to call back.

6. **Computer, video game, TV, stereo use:** _____ will maintain reasonable levels of volume and turn down sound equipment when asked. Computer use is allowed for the following purposes:

No use of the computer will be allowed for _____ .
Video game use will be limited to no more than _____ minutes per day on school days/evenings and _____ on other days. TV viewing will be no more than _____ on school days, and _____ on other days. The types of TV programs _____ may watch will be determined by parent(s).

7. **Health and self-care:** _____ will shower/bathe _____ (frequency), wear clean clothes to school and other public places, wash and groom his/her hair and nails (or with help if very young), brush teeth _____ (times), eat nutritious foods, and will not take any drugs without specific knowledge and permission of parent(s), use cigarettes, alcohol, or experiment with any substances that may be harmful.

8. **Helping tasks:** Each family member will have responsibility for the completion of certain tasks necessary for the functioning of our family. _____ will be responsible for completing the following tasks before the designated deadline and will follow the specific steps for satisfactory completion of those tasks given by parent(s) on index cards.

TASK	TO BE DONE BY:	
a. _____	_____ (day)	_____(time)
b. _____	_____ (day)	_____(time)
c. _____	_____ (day)	_____(time)
d. _____	_____ (day)	_____(time)

[Resources]

Baumrind, D. "Rearing Competent Children." *Child Development Today and Tomorrow*, W. Damon, ed., pp. 349–378. San Francisco: Jossey-Bass, 1989.

Baumrind, D. "The Influence of Parenting Style on Adolescent Competence and Substance Use." *Journal of Early Adolescence*, *11*(1), 56–95, 1991.

Darling, N., and L. Steinberg. "Parenting Style as Context: An Integrative Model." *Psychological Bulletin*, *113* (3), pp. 487–496, 1993.

Maccoby, E. E., and J. A. Martin. "Socialization in the Context of the Family: Parent–Child Interaction." *Handbook of Child Psychology: Vol. 4. Socialization, Personality, and Social Development*, 4th ed., P. H. Mussen (ed.) and E. M. Hetherington (vol. ed.), pp. 1–101. New York: John Wiley & Sons, 1983.

Thomas, A., and S. Chess. *Temperament and Development*. New York: Brunner/Mazel, 1977.

CHILD TEMPERAMENT

New York University Child Study Center, http://www.aboutourkids .org/

Family and Consumer Sciences Agent, Hardin County, Ohio State University Extension, The Ohio State University, http://www//ohioline.osu.edu/

CHILD DEVELOPMENT AND BEHAVIOR PROBLEMS

Murphy, Timothy, and Loriann Hoff Oberlin. *The Angry Child: Regaining Control When Your Child Is Out of Control.* New York: Three Rivers Press, 1993.

National Institute of Child Health and Human Development, http://www.nichd.nih.gov/

National Institutes of Mental Health: Child and Adolescent Mental Health, http://www.nimh.nih.gov/healthinformation /childmenu.cfm

Tufts University Child & Family WebGuide, http://www.cfw.tufts .edu/

ADHD

Alexander-Roberts, Colleen. *The ADHD Parenting Handbook: Practical Advice for Parents from Parents.* Lanham, Md.: Taylor Trade Publishing, 1994.

CHADD (Children and Adults with Attention-Deficit Hyperactivity Disorder), http://www.chadd.org/

Rief, Sandra F. *How to Reach and Teach ADD/ADHD Children: Practical Techniques, Strategies, and Interventions for Helping*

Children with Attention Problems and Hyperactivity. San Francisco: Jossey-Bass, 1993.

SENSORY INTEGRATIVE DYSFUNCTION

Kranowitz, Carol Stock. *The Out-of-Sync Child Has Fun: Activities for Kids with Sensory Integration Dysfunction.* New York: Perigee Books, 2003.

Sensory Integration International: 1514 Cabrillo Avenue, Torrance, Calif., 90501.

Smith, Karen A., and Karen R. Gouze. *The Sensory-Sensitive Child: Practical Solutions for Out-of-Bounds Behavior.* New York: HarperResource, 2004.

[Index]

[Index]

[About the Author]

Mary-Elaine Jacobsen, Psy.D., earned a bachelor's degree in elementary education from the University of Minnesota. She taught for five years, where she advocated for the gifted and developed forward-thinking, specialized curricula for gifted students. She subsequently obtained a Master's degree and Doctorate in Clinical Psychology from the University of St. Thomas, in St. Paul, Minnesota. She was the chief psychologist for the Amherst Wilder Child Guidance Clinic and is now an associate professor of psychology at Salem College in North Carolina.

In her 1999 breakthrough book—*Liberating Everyday Genius: A Revolutionary Guide for Identifying and Mastering Your Exceptional Gifts*, she pioneered the first comprehensive book that explained the personality factors and life issues of gifted adults, with many practical suggestions. It remains the only book of its kind in print. The softcover version was published in 2000 under a new title, *The Gifted Adult*, which continues to sell worldwide. A Spanish version was released in 2001. Nearly every day since the publication of the book, Dr. Jacobsen has received letters, calls, and e-mails from gifted readers across the United States and from more than fifteen other countries on every continent except Antarctica. As a frequent guest speaker, trainer, and workshop provider, teachers, parents of gifted children, and many unidentified gifted adults, repeatedly stress how her insights and strategies have better prepared them to understand and guide their gifted children and/or themselves toward success. With a thorough appreciation of the developmental process and special challenges of the gifted, her practical suggestions quickly help parents and teachers avoid common mistakes.

As the director of OmegaPoint Resources for the Gifted and Talented, Dr. Jacobsen counsels gifted children and their parents, as well as gifted/talented adults. She provides specialized consultation services to schools, businesses, educators, physicians, executives, and professionals in the arts here and abroad. She is often called upon to train executive groups in gifted team building, gifted leadership identification, and leadership development. From 2001 to 2003 she was also a consultant to the media, and regular guest on her local NBC affiliate's *Today* show.

Dr. Jacobsen has published numerous articles on giftedness and child development, and has served on the Board for the Counseling Division of the National Association for Gifted Children. She is a contributing editor for the *Roeper Review: A Journal of Gifted Education*, and a reviewer for the *Journal of Secondary Gifted Education*. She is also the founder and chairperson of the newly founded *International Society for Gifted Adults and Child Advocates, ISGAA*.

Dr. Jacobsen is also developing a psychological testing instrument for the identification of emerging gifted leaders. She has raised three gifted children who (she is relieved to report) are now successfully developing their exceptional gifts as young adults in medicine, film technology, and international security, in North Carolina, California, and England.